Neoliberalism: A Very Short Introduction

VERY SHORT INTRODUCTIONS are for anyone wanting a stimulating and accessible way into a new subject. They are written by experts, and have been translated into more than 45 different languages.

The Series began in 1995, and now covers a wide variety of topics in every discipline. The VSI library currently contains over 650 volumes—a *Very Short Introduction* to everything from Psychology and Philosophy of Science to American History and Relativity—and continues to grow in every subject area.

Very Short Introductions available now:

Available soon:

For more information visit our website

www.oup.com/vsi/

Manfred B. Steger and Ravi K. Roy

# NEOLIBERALISM

## A Very Short Introduction

### SECOND EDITION

OXFORD
UNIVERSITY PRESS

# OXFORD

UNIVERSITY PRESS

Great Clarendon Street, Oxford, OX2 6DP,
United Kingdom

Oxford University Press is a department of the University of Oxford.
It furthers the University's objective of excellence in research, scholarship,
and education by publishing worldwide. Oxford is a registered trade mark of
Oxford University Press in the UK and in certain other countries

First edition published 2010
This edition published 2021

Impression: 1

Published in the United States of America by Oxford University Press
198 Madison Avenue, New York, NY 10016, United States of America

British Library Cataloguing in Publication Data
Data available

Library of Congress Control Number: 2019951497

ISBN 978-0-19-884967-4

Printed in Great Britain by
Ashford Colour Press Ltd, Gosport, Hampshire

# Contents

# Preface

Our 21st-century world is a fundamentally interdependent place. Globalization has expanded, intensified, and accelerated social relations and consciousness across world-time and world-space. The digital revolution has served as a catalyst for the creation of sprawling information and communication networks that—for better or worse—enmesh individuals, states, and businesses alike. Ubiquitous transnational terrorist cells have targeted symbols of secular power and prompted Western political leaders to declare a perpetual 'global war on terror'. Global climate change and global pandemics like the 2020 coronavirus outbreak have become frightening realities, forcing countries to work out a transnational strategy aimed at preventing a catastrophe of planetary proportions. Inequality among nations has accelerated; global migration flows have increased; and large-scale trade wars involving superpowers like the United States and China have strained international relations.

Obviously, we live in unsettled times. Triumphalist voices who once saw the collapse of Soviet communism as the end of history and the beginning of the unchallenged rule of American-style free-market capitalism have recently been caught off guard by the tremendous appeal of the populist promise to return to the safety and stability of the bygone era of autonomous nation states. Wavering between globalist expansion and nationalist retrenchment, the world has turned into an ideological battlefield where new ideas packaged for the social media vie for the hearts and minds of a global audience.

Neoliberalism is one of these contending 'isms'. The term was first coined in post-First World War Germany by a small circle of ideologically moderate economists and legal scholars affiliated with the academic Freiburg School to refer to their comprehensive programme of reviving the classical liberal ideal of minimal state interference in the economy. Decades later, in the 1970s, a group of Latin American economists adopted *neoliberalismo* as a buzzword for their more aggressive pro-market agenda. Soon thereafter, left-leaning critics in the global South were imbuing neoliberalism with pejorative rhetoric, associating the term with cut-throat capitalism imposed by wealthy corporations and rich governments in the West.

In the late 1980s and early 1990s, leftist activists and academics alike began equating neoliberalism with the Washington Consensus—a set of economic institutions and policies alleged to have been designed by the United States to globalize American capitalism and its associated consumerist culture. Other critics dismissed neoliberalism as an opaque catchphrase invented by the radical Left or right-wing economic nationalists for the purpose of downgrading the intellectual achievements of mainstream neoclassical economists and more ardent free-market libertarians such as Nobel Prize winners Friedrich von Hayek and Milton Friedman. Still others saw it as a postmodern version of quaint 18th-century laissez-faire talk glorifying individual self-interest, economic efficiency, and unbridled entrepreneurship. In spite of these diverging meanings, however, the term neoliberalism has stuck in the public mind.

In its heyday during the 1980s and 1990s, neoliberalism bestrode the world like a colossus. Personified by Anglo-American politicians like Ronald Reagan, Margaret Thatcher, Bill Clinton, and Tony

Blair, it confronted countries in the global South with harsh rules and conditions for their economic development. Showing itself to be a remarkably versatile and adaptable creature, neoliberalism ate its way into the heart of the communist world. It even managed to charm post-Mao Chinese leaders like Deng Xiaoping, Jiang Zemin, and Hu Jintao into adopting 'socialism with Chinese characteristics'. In the process, Chinese communism assumed large parts of its supposed capitalist nemesis. Over the ensuing decades, significant parts of the neoliberal agenda were adopted by such different figures as Manmohan Singh, Junichiro Koizumi, John Howard, George W. Bush, Barack Obama, and Xi Jinping. But not one of these political leaders ever publicly embraced this ambiguous label—although they all shared an affinity for neoliberal policies aimed at deregulating national economies, liberalizing international trade, privatizing state-owned enterprises, downsizing government, cutting taxes, and creating a single global market.

The 2008–9 Global Financial Crisis (GFC) and the related European Sovereign Debt Crisis (ESDC) triggered a decade of economic volatility and insecurity that boosted the fortunes of the 1 per cent while saddling the 99 per cent with stagnant wages and precarious work. As a result of these troubling developments, major components of neoliberalism have been attacked by antiglobalist populists such as Donald Trump, Nigel Farage, Boris Johnson, Viktor Órban, Vladimir Putin, Jair Bolsonaro, and Marine Le Pen. The astonishing political success of these nationalist leaders—especially in such unlikely places as the USA and the UK—made concerned commentators wonder whether the international post-war liberal order was teetering at the brink of collapse. At the start of the 2020s, however, it has become clear that segments of neoliberalism have actually been embraced by these very populist leaders who have staked their entire political career on denouncing it.

Is neoliberalism doomed or will it regain its former glory? What are the major types of neoliberalism and how did they evolve over the decades? Might new versions of neoliberalism succeed in drowning out the siren song of national populism and its nostalgic longing for a return to the good old days of territorial sovereignty and national greatness?

Responding to these crucial questions, this book has been designed to introduce readers to the origins, evolution, and core ideas of neoliberalism by examining its concrete manifestations in countries and regions around the world. Our historically sensitive journey into these variants will show that although neoliberals across the globe share a common belief in the power of self-regulating free markets to create a better world, their doctrine comes in different hues and multiple applications. Reaganomics, for example, is not exactly the same as Thatcherism. Bill Clinton's brand of market globalism diverges in some respects from Tony Blair's Third Way. Barack Obama's reformist neoliberalism differs from the austerity-oriented neoliberal framework that dominated the EU after the GFC. Political elites in the global South (often educated at the elite universities of the North) have learned to fit the tenets of the Washington Consensus to match their own local contexts and idiosyncratic political objectives. Thus, it makes sense to think of our subject in the plural—*neoliberalisms*—rather than confining it to a single monolithic manifestation cast in the Anglo-American mould.

While neoliberalism has adapted to specific environments, problems, and opportunities, it has struggled to mount an effective counterattack against the current populist explosion. Yet, new technocentric and futuristic versions of neoliberalism are being assembled as we speak. The main ideas, policies, and modes of governance fuelling *all* neoliberal projects—old and new—lie at the heart of this volume. Carrying out our publisher's objective to keep this introduction *very short*, we offer a general discussion based on selective examples. Our main purpose is to present an accessible and informative—but bare—outline of a rich and complex phenomenon. Readers who have digested the materials offered here and feel prepared to delve more deeply into our subject are advised to consult the concluding reference section.

We appreciate the support of our colleagues and friends at the University of Hawai'i at Mānoa, Western Sydney University, Southern Utah University, and The W. Edwards Deming Institute©. Jenny Nugee, Luciana O'Flaherty, and their able VSI team at Oxford University Press have been wonderful to work with. But most of all, we wish to thank our respective families for their enduring love and support. Perle, Joan, Nicole, and Yianna, this book is for you! Many people have contributed to making this a better book; its remaining shortcomings are our sole responsibility.

# List of illustrations

# List of figures

# List of maps

# Abbreviations

| | |
|---|---|
| **AAPI** | Asian Americans and Pacific Islanders |
| **AI** | artificial intelligence |
| **ARRA** | American Recovery and Reinvestment Act (2009) |
| **AT&T** | American Telephone and Telegraph |
| **BITs** | bilateral investment treaties |
| **CCP** | Chinese Communist Party |
| **CIA** | Central Intelligence Agency |
| **DLC** | Democratic Leadership Council |
| **ECB** | European Central Bank |
| **EESA** | Emergency Economic Stabilization Act |
| **EO** | Executive Order |
| **EPA** | Environmental Protection Agency |
| **ERCA** | Economic Growth, Regulatory Relief and Consumer Protection Act |
| **ERM** | Exchange Rate Mechanism |
| **ESDC** | European Sovereign Debt Crisis |
| **EU** | European Union |
| **FDI** | foreign direct investment |
| **FDR** | Franklin D. Roosevelt |
| **FTA** | Free Trade Agreement |
| **FTAA** | Free Trade Area of the Americas |
| **G-7** | Group of Seven |
| **G20** | Group of Twenty |
| **GATT** | General Agreement on Tariffs and Trade |

| | |
|---|---|
| **GDP** | gross domestic product |
| **GFC** | Global Financial Crisis |
| **GJM** | global justice movement |
| **GOP** | Grand Old Party; American Republican Party |
| **GRH** | Gramm–Rudman–Hollings Deficit Reduction Initiative |
| **HDI** | Human Development Index |
| **HIPCs** | heavily indebted poor countries |
| **ICT** | information and communications technology |
| **IFIs** | international financial institutions |
| **IMF** | International Monetary Fund |
| **ISIS** | Islamic State of Iraq and Syria |
| **LDP** | Liberal Democratic Party (Japan) |
| **MITI** | Ministry of International Trade and Industry (Japan) |
| **MOF** | Ministry of Finance (Japan) |
| **MTFS** | medium term financial strategy |
| **NAFTA** | North American Free Trade Agreement |
| **NATO** | North Atlantic Treaty Organization |
| **NHS** | (UK) National Health Service |
| **NPM** | new public management |
| **NPP** | New Patriotic Party (Ghana) |
| **OBOR** | One Belt One Road (Chinese infrastructure initiative) |
| **PPP** | public–private partnerships |
| **PRI** | Institutional Revolutionary Party (Mexico) |
| **S&L** | Savings and Loans industry |
| **SAPRI** | Structural Adjustment Review Initiative |
| **SAPs** | structural adjustment programmes |
| **SCP** | Soviet Communist Party |
| **SEZs** | special enterprise zones |
| **SOEs** | state-owned enterprises |
| **STEM** | science, technology, engineering, & mathematics |
| **TARP** | Troubled Asset Relief Program |
| **TCJA** | Tax Cuts and Jobs Act (2017) |
| **TNCs** | transnational corporations |

| | |
|---|---|
| **TPP** | Trans-Pacific Partnership |
| **TRIPs** | trade-related aspects of intellectual property rights |
| **TQM** | total quality management |
| **USMCA** | United States-Mexico-Canada (Trade) Agreement |
| **US** | United States (of America) |
| **USSR** | Union of Soviet Socialist Republics |
| **WC** | Washington Consensus |
| **WEF** | World Economic Forum |
| **WSF** | World Social Forum |
| **WTO** | World Trade Organization |

# Chapter 1
# What's 'neo' about liberalism?

## Liberalism old and new

At a joint 2018 press conference with Japan's Prime Minister Shinzō Abe, US President Donald Trump (see Illustration 1)—the world's most influential advocate of trade protectionism and tighter immigration restrictions—delivered a bold sales pitch that seemed to defy his national populist principles:

> There's never been a better time to invest in the United States. Thanks to our massive tax cuts, historic deregulation, a strong trade policy, which has just really begun—because I will tell you over the years it has been an extraordinarily weak trade policy—the opening of American energy, and a return to the rule of law, our economy is absolutely booming. Best it's ever been.

The US president's odd mixture of two central pillars of neoliberalism—the deregulation of the economy and massive tax cuts—with a central tenet of economic nationalism—trade protectionism (camouflaged as 'strong trade policy')—attests to his infamous ideational inconsistency. In addition, as we shall discuss in the final chapter, Trump's obvious incoherence also demonstrates that major parts of the free-market thinking that had dominated the world for three decades are alive and well

**1. US President Donald Trump (1946–) speaking at a joint press conference with Japan's Prime Minister Shinzō Abe (1954–), 7 June 2018.**

today—and even championed by the resurgent forces of national populism.

On the other hand, Trump's contradictory remarks suggest that the unflagging 'globalist' pro-market vision that had been originally shaped and disseminated by Ronald Reagan and Margaret Thatcher is no longer at the centre of the reconfigured Anglo-American conservative parties. In fact, at the high-profile 2019 National Conservatism Conference in Washington, DC, speaker after speaker denounced neoliberalism. Some, like Oren Cass, a senior fellow at the conservative Manhattan Institute, even went so far as to eviscerate the entire classical liberal tradition by flatly stating that 'the market does not work'.

To be sure, the object of Cass's criticism—the neoliberal ideal of the self-regulating market as the main engine powering the individual's rational pursuit of wealth—had been a core tenet of economists since the late 18th century. Opposed to the mercantilist doctrine associated with European monarchs who exercised almost total control over the economy in their efforts to amass large quantities of gold for largely bellicose purposes, classical liberals like Adam Smith and David Ricardo preached the virtues of the free-market and laissez-faire economics (see Box 1 and Illustration 2).

Smith has been credited with creating the Scottish Enlightenment image of *homo economicus*—the view that human beings are social creatures who seek to maximize their individual material self-interests through voluntary exchange with others in a free market. According to this view, economic and political matters are largely separable, with economics claiming a superior status because it operates best without government interference under a harmonious system of natural laws. Thus, the state is to refrain from 'interfering' with the economic activities of self-interested citizens and instead use its power to guarantee open economic exchange. At the same time, however, Smith was fully aware of the potential for market failure. Indeed, he laid out a very carefully crafted argument on the need for a very strong, though narrow,

## Box 1 Classical liberalism and the Enlightenment

Classical liberalism arose in tandem with the Enlightenment movement of the late 17th and the 18th centuries which proclaimed reason as the foundation of individual freedom. Enlightenment thinkers like John Locke (1632–1704) argued that in the 'state of nature', all men were free and equal, therefore possessing inalienable rights independent of the laws of any government or authority. Naturally endowed with the right to life, liberty, and property, humans could legitimately establish only *limited* governments whose chief task consisted of securing and protecting these individual rights, especially private property.

2. Adam Smith (1723–90).

place for government intervention, especially in the cases of monopolies or where private firms attempted to manipulate and distort the market.

Ricardo's theory of comparative advantage became the gospel of modern free traders. He argued that free trade amounted to a win–win situation for all trading partners involved because it allowed each country to specialize in the production of those commodities for which it had a comparative advantage. For example, if Portugal could produce wine more cheaply than England, and England could produce cloth more cheaply than Portugal, then both countries would benefit from specialization and trade. In fact, Ricardo suggested that benefits from specialization and trade would accrue even if one country had an absolute advantage in producing all of the products traded. Politically, Ricardo's theory amounted to a powerful argument against government interference with trade. Indeed, it was used by 19th-century liberals like Richard Cobden as a formidable ideological weapon in the struggle to repeal the protectionist Corn Laws in England.

Classical liberals saw producers and consumers as equal actors who pursued their own discrete material needs and wants as they saw fit. Dedicated to the protection of private property and the legal enforcement of contracts, classical liberals argued that the 'invisible hand' of the market was the most efficient and effective mechanism for allocating resources and promoting greater equality within a country as well as facilitating peaceful commercial intercourse among nations. Their ideas proved to be a potent force in fomenting the great 18th-century revolutions that toppled royal dynasties, separated church and state, and shattered the dogmas of mercantilism. For most of the 19th century, the heirs of classical liberalism sought to convince people that bad economic times reflected some form of government failure—usually too much state interference resulting in distorted price signals and propensities for moral hazard. How could there be such a thing as market failure, they reasoned, if markets—properly shielded from the meddling state—were by nature incapable of failing?

But the turbulent 20th century soon cast a dark cloud on these tenets of classical liberalism. It wasn't until the 1980s that neoliberals managed to bring back some of these quaint ideas—albeit dressed in new garments. So what happened in the intervening period? The story is well known. The fury and longevity of the Great Depression convinced leading economic thinkers like John Maynard Keynes and Karl Polanyi that government was much more than a mere nightwatchman—the role assigned to the state by classical liberals (see Illustration 3).

At the same time, however, Keynes and his new breed of egalitarian liberals disagreed with Marxists who saw the persistence of economic crises as evidence for the coming collapse of capitalism and the victory of a revolutionary proletariat that had seen through the ideological distortions of the ruling bourgeoisie: never again would workers fall into the clever trap of accepting their own exploitation in the name of high-sounding liberal ideals like freedom, opportunity, and hard work. Seeking to prevent revolution by means of economic reform, egalitarian liberals like Prime Minister Clement Attlee and President Franklin D. Roosevelt remained staunch defenders of individual autonomy and property rights. And yet, they criticized classical liberalism for its inability to recognize that modern capitalism had to be subjected to certain regulations and controls by a strong secular state.

Keynes, in particular, advocated massive government spending in a time of economic crisis to create new jobs and lift consumer spending. Thus, he challenged classical liberal beliefs that the market mechanism would naturally correct itself in the event of an economic crisis and return to an equilibrium at full employment. Keynes linked unemployment to a shortage of private capital investment and spending in the economy. For this

3. John Maynard Keynes (1883–1946).

shortfall, he blamed short-sighted and avaricious investors, whose speculative investments had destabilized the market. Committed to the market principle but opposed to the unfettered market, Keynesianism even called for some state ownership of

## Box 2  Keynesian macroeconomics

John Maynard Keynes's literary masterpiece, *The General Theory of Employment, Interest and Money*, was published in 1936 at the height of the Great Depression. The book gained instant prominence because it successfully challenged classical liberal ideas about how modern economies worked. Keynesian ideas proved to be crucial in the development of the theoretical framework of macroeconomics. This new field proclaimed that it was possible for national governments to aggregate data and predict economic crises in advance of their occurrence, thus proposing the use of various policies to intervene in and make adjustments to the economy. Specifically, governments were to increase public spending during economic recessions in order to spur growth and reduce spending during periods of boom in order to keep inflation in check. Keynesian ideas dominated macroeconomics until the rise of neoliberal doctrines in the early 1970s.

crucial national enterprises like railways or energy companies (see Box 2).

Keynes led the British delegation at the 1944 Bretton Woods Conference in the United States, which established the post-war international economic order and its international economic institutions. The International Monetary Fund (IMF) was created to administer the international monetary system. The International Bank for Reconstruction and Development, later known as the World Bank, was initially designed to provide loans for Europe's post-war reconstruction. During the 1950s, however, its purpose was expanded to fund various industrial projects in developing countries around the world. Finally, the General Agreement on Tariffs and Trade (GATT) was established in 1947 as a global trade organization charged with fashioning and enforcing multilateral trade agreements. In 1995, the World Trade Organization (WTO) was founded as the successor organization to GATT and subsequently became the focal point of intense public controversy over its neoliberal design of free trade agreements.

The political applications of Keynesian ideas inspired what some economists called the 'golden age of controlled capitalism', which lasted roughly from 1945 to 1975 (see Box 3). The American New Deal and Great Society programmes spearheaded by FDR and President Lyndon Johnson were modelled on the much-admired

## Box 3  The golden age of controlled capitalism in the United States

The capitalist economy was based on mass production. Mass production was profitable because a large middle class had enough money to purchase what could be produced in large volume. The middle class had the money because the profits from mass production were divided up between big business and their suppliers, retailers, and employees. The bargaining power of labour was enhanced and enforced by favourable government action. Almost a third of the American workforce belonged to a union and benefited from steady wage rises delivered by means of legally guaranteed collective bargaining processes. Economic benefits were spread across the nation—to farmers, veterans, smaller towns, and small business—through regulatory mechanisms applying to railroads, telephones, utilities, and small business as well as generous subsidies in the form of price supports, highways, and federal loans.

Source: Robert Reich, *Supercapitalism: The Transformation of Business, Democracy, and Everyday Life* (Knopf, 2008), p. 17.

model of Swedish social democracy, and the British version of social welfarism launched in 1945 by Prime Minister Clement Attlee. The global appeal of Keynesianism culminated in a broad political consensus among Western nations that led some pundits to proclaim the 'end of ideology'. Under the Keynesian economic regime, national governments exercised significant control over money flows in and out of their territories. In addition, progressive taxes on wealthy individuals and profitable corporations led to the expansion of the welfare state. Moreover, rising wages and increased social services in the wealthy countries of the global North offered workers entry into the middle class.

Even US President Richard Nixon, a conservative Republican, proclaimed as late as 1970 that 'we are all Keynesians now'. It was the Keynesian advocacy of an interventionist state and regulated markets that gave liberalism its modern economic meaning: a doctrine favouring a large, active government, regulation of industry, high taxes for the rich, and extensive social welfare programmes for all.

In the three decades following the Second World War, modern egalitarian liberalism delivered spectacular economic growth rates, high wages, low inflation, and unprecedented levels of material well-being and social security. But this golden age of controlled capitalism ground to a halt with the severe economic crises of the 1970s. In response to such unprecedented calamities as oil shocks that quadrupled the price of petrol overnight, the simultaneous occurrence of runaway inflation and rising unemployment ('stagflation'), and falling corporate profits, an entirely new breed of liberals sought a way forward by recasting some of the core elements of classical liberalism under the novel conditions of globalization.

These neoliberals subscribed to a common set of ideological and political principles dedicated to the worldwide spread of an economic model emphasizing free markets and free trade. And yet, they emphasized different parts of their theory according to their particular social contexts. Worshipped by their followers and detested by the Keynesians, neoliberals succeeded in the early 1980s in setting the world's economic and political agenda for the next quarter-century. As we shall discuss in Chapter 2, they argued that crippling government regulation, exorbitant public spending, and high tariff barriers to international trade had been responsible for creating conditions that led to high inflation and poor economic growth throughout the industrial countries in the 1970s. Once this premise became widely accepted, it was the logical next step to claim that these factors remained the major impediment to successful economic development in the global South.

Thus was born a global neoliberal development agenda based primarily on so-called structural adjustment programmes (SAPs) and international free-trade agreements. As we shall see in Chapters 3 and 4, powerful economic institutions like the International Monetary Fund (IMF) and the World Bank imposed their neoliberal agenda on heavily indebted developing countries in return for much-needed loans. The 1991 demise of the Soviet Union and the acceleration of market-oriented reforms in communist China led to the unprecedented dominance of the neoliberal model in the 1990s.

As we noted in the Preface, however, during the last decade neoliberalism has come under a series of criticisms. The 2008–9 GFC triggered a series of challenges to the still dominant free-market paradigm that boosted the political fortunes of national-populism around the world—a development most spectacularly reflected in 2016's pro-Brexit referendum in the UK and the Trump election victory in the same year. But before we can appreciate the full magnitude of the threats facing neoliberalism, we must familiarize ourselves with its various dimensions, varieties, and policy applications. Let us commence our journey with a brief consideration of its core ideas and principles.

## The four dimensions of neoliberalism

Neoliberalism is a rather broad and general concept referring to an economic model or paradigm that rose to prominence in the 1980s. Built upon the classical liberal ideal of the self-regulating market, neoliberalism comes in several strands and variations. Perhaps the best way to conceptualize neoliberalism is to think of it as four intertwined manifestations: (1) an ideology; (2) a mode of governance; (3) a policy package; (4) a particular form of capitalism. Let us carefully unpack these fundamental domains.

Ideologies are systems of widely shared ideas and patterned beliefs that are accepted as truth by significant groups in society. Such isms serve as indispensable conceptual maps or mental models because they guide people through the complexity of their political worlds. They not only offer a more or less coherent picture of the world as it is, but also as it ought to be. In doing so, ideologies organize their core ideas into fairly simple truth-claims that encourage people to act in certain ways. These claims are assembled by codifiers of ideologies to legitimize certain political interests and to defend or challenge dominant power structures. The codifiers of neoliberalism are global power elites that include managers and executives of large transnational corporations, corporate lobbyists, influential journalists and public-relations specialists, intellectuals writing for a large public audience, celebrities and top entertainers, state bureaucrats, and politicians.

Serving as the chief advocates of neoliberalism, these individuals saturate the public discourse with idealized images of a consumerist, free-market world. Skilfully interacting with the media to sell their preferred version of a single global marketplace to the public, they portray globalizing markets in a positive light as an indispensable tool for the realization of a better world. Such market visions of globalization pervade public opinion and political choices in many parts of the world. Indeed, neoliberal decision-makers function as expert designers of an attractive ideological container for their market-friendly political agenda. Their ideological claims are laced with references to global economic interdependence rooted in the principles of free-market capitalism: global trade and financial markets, worldwide flows of goods, services, and labour, transnational corporations, offshore financial centres, and so on. For this reason, it makes sense to think of neoliberalism as a rather economistic ideology, which, not unlike its arch-rival Marxism, puts the production and exchange of material goods at the heart of the human experience.

The second dimension of neoliberalism refers to what the French social thinker Michel Foucault called 'governmentalities'—certain modes of governance based on particular premises, logics, and power relations. A neoliberal governmentality is rooted in entrepreneurial values such as competitiveness, self-interest, and decentralization. It celebrates individual empowerment and the devolution of central state power to smaller localized units. Such a neoliberal mode of governance adopts the self-regulating free market as the model for proper government. Rather than operating along more traditional lines of pursuing the public good (rather than profits) by enhancing civil society and social justice, neoliberals call for the employment of governmental technologies that are taken from the world of business and commerce: mandatory development of strategic plans and risk-management schemes oriented toward the creation of surpluses; cost–benefit analyses and other efficiency calculations; the shrinking of political governance (so-called 'best-practice governance'); the setting of quantitative targets; the close monitoring of outcomes; the creation of highly individualized, performance-based work plans; and the introduction of rational choice models that internalize and thus normalize market-oriented behaviour. Neoliberal modes of governance encourage the transformation of bureaucratic mentalities into entrepreneurial identities where government workers see themselves no longer as public servants and guardians of a qualitatively defined public good but as self-interested actors responsible to the market and contributing to the monetary success of slimmed-down state enterprises.

As we discuss in Chapter 2, a novel model of public administration known as new public management (NPM) took the world's state bureaucracies by storm in the 1980s. Operationalizing the neoliberal mode of governance for public servants, the NPM redefined citizens as 'customers' or 'clients' and encouraged administrators to cultivate an entrepreneurial spirit. If private enterprises must nurture innovation and enhance productivity in order to survive in the competitive marketplace, new public management advocates argued, why shouldn't government workers embrace neoliberal ideals to improve the public sector? In the 1990s, US Vice-President Al Gore famously utilized new public management principles to subject various government agencies to a National Performance Review whose declared objective was to cut government waste and increase administrative efficiency, effectiveness, and accountability.

Third, neoliberalism manifests itself as a concrete set of public policies expressed in what we like to call the D-L-P Formula: (1) **D**eregulation (of the economy); (2) **L**iberalization (of trade and industry); and (3) **P**rivatization (of state-owned enterprises). Related policy measures include massive tax cuts (especially for businesses and high-income earners); reduction of social services and welfare programmes; replacing welfare with 'workfare'; use of interest rates by independent central banks to keep inflation in check (even at the risk of increasing unemployment); the downsizing of government; tax havens for domestic and foreign corporations willing to invest in designated economic zones; new commercial urban spaces shaped by market imperatives; anti-unionization drives in the name of enhancing productivity and 'labour flexibility'; removal of controls on global financial and trade flows; regional and global integration of national economies; and the creation of new political institutions, think tanks, and practices designed to promote the neoliberal paradigm. As we shall see in Chapter 2, so-called 'neoconservative' initiatives often supported the neoliberal policy agenda in pursuit of shared political objectives. In turn, many neoliberals embraced conservative values, especially 'family values', tough law enforcement, and a strong military. The nearly universal adoption of at least some parts of this policy package in the 1990s reflected the global power of the ideological claims of neoliberalism.

Fourth, as economist David Kotz emphasizes, neoliberalism is a particular form of free-market capitalism that replaced the form of controlled capitalism that preceded it. While capitalism has retained certain defining features since its 17th-century origin as trade capitalism, it assumed a series of distinct social structures of accumulation over time. Each form of capitalism has its own internal coherence, a set of corresponding political and economic institutions, and dominant ideas that reinforce people's belief in the naturalness of these changing social structures of accumulation. Transitions from one institutional form of capitalism to the next occur as a result of general economic crises such as the Great Depression and lead to the restructuring of capitalism. As we discussed above, the new neoliberal form of capitalism arose in response to the severe crises of the 1970s and manifested itself in a concrete set of pro-market institutions and policies.

As we noted in the preface, Chapters 2–5 will pay attention to all four dimensions of neoliberalism, including an examination of concrete policy applications in different settings around the world. But let us first complete our clarification of conceptual matters with a brief review of the major economic theories that fuelled the rise of neoliberalism in the late 1970s.

## The intellectual origins of neoliberalism

Although neoliberalism comes in several varieties, one can find an early systematic formulation of its economic principles in the philosophical ethos of the Mont Pelerin Society. Founded in 1947 by Friedrich August von Hayek, an influential member of the early 20th-century Austrian School of Economics, the Society attracted like-minded intellectuals committed to strengthening the principles and practice of a free society by studying the workings and virtues of market-oriented economic systems. Vowing to stem what they saw as the rising tide of collectivism—be it Marxism or even less radical forms of state-centred planning—Hayek and his colleagues sought to revive classical liberalism in their attempt to challenge the dominance of Keynesian ideas.

A great believer in the free market's spontaneous ability to function as a self-regulating and knowledge-generating engine of human freedom and ingenuity, Hayek considered most forms of state intervention in the economy as ominous milestones on the 'road to serfdom' leading to new forms of government-engineered despotism. His economic theory was anchored in the notion of undistorted price mechanisms that served to share and synchronize local and personal knowledge, thus allowing individual members of society to achieve diverse ends without state interference. For Hayek, economic freedom could never be subordinated to political liberty and confined to the narrow sphere of material production. Rather, it was a profoundly political and moral force that shaped all other aspects of a free and open society. Surprisingly, however, the members of the Mont Pelerin Society occasionally strayed into conservative ideological territory by emphasizing the limits of human rationality and the importance of time-honoured values and traditions in the constitution of human societies (see Box 4).

The neoliberal principles advocated by Hayek's Mont Pelerin Society greatly influenced the American economist Milton Friedman, winner of the 1976 Nobel Prize. The charismatic leader of the Chicago School of Economics (based at the University of Chicago), Friedman had an influential hand in guiding neoliberalism from constituting a mere minority view in the 1950s to becoming the ruling economic orthodoxy in the 1990s.

### Box 4 Libertarianism

Often associated with the economic doctrines of Friedrich von Hayek (1899–1992) and Milton Friedman (1912–2006), libertarianism is a perspective hostile to government intervention. While sharing general agreement with mainstream liberalism on the primacy of individual liberty, most libertarians are strictly opposed to other liberal values such as equality, solidarity, and social responsibility. Rejecting many modern government interventionist practices as illegitimate for their reliance on coercive policies, libertarians subscribe to the utopian ideal of a loose society of autonomous individuals engaged in strictly voluntary forms of exchange. Indeed, more extreme libertarians go even so far as to demand the wholesale abolition of the state.

Focusing on inflation as the most dangerous economic outcome of state interference—such as price controls imposed by Keynesian governments to guarantee low-income earners access to basic commodities—Friedman developed his theory of monetarism. It posited that only the self-regulating free market allowed for the right number of goods at correct prices produced by workers paid at wage levels determined by the free market. By the early 1980s, monetarists like Friedman insisted that slaying the dragon of inflation required that central banks like the US Federal Reserve pursue anti-inflationary policies that kept the supply and demand for money at equilibrium. In short, tight monetary goals should take precedence over fiscal policy (taxation and redistribution policies) devised by 'big government'.

As we shall see in Chapters 2–5, neoliberalism soon spread to other parts of the world—often by means of so-called 'shock therapies' devised by prominent neoliberal economists. Examples include Chile after General Augusto Pinochet's 1973 CIA-supported

## Box 5  The Washington Consensus

The Washington Consensus is often viewed as synonymous with neoliberalism. Coined in the 1980s by the free-market economist John Williamson, the term refers to the lowest common denominator of policy advice directed at mostly Latin American countries by the IMF, the World Bank, and other Washington-based international economic institutions and think tanks. In the 1990s, it became the global framework for economic development. In exchange for much-needed loans and debt-restructuring schemes, governments in the global South were required to adhere to the Washington Consensus by following its ten-point programme:

1. A guarantee of fiscal discipline, and a curb to budget deficit.
2. A reduction of public expenditure, particularly in the military and public administration.
3. Tax reform, aiming at the creation of a system with a broad base and with effective enforcement.
4. Financial liberalization, with interest rates determined by the market.
5. Competitive exchange rates, to assist export-led growth.
6. Trade liberalization, coupled with the abolition of import licensing and a reduction of tariffs.
7. Promotion of foreign direct investment.
8. Privatization of state enterprises, leading to efficient management and improved performance.
9. Deregulation of the economy.
10. Protection of property rights.

coup, the economic transformation of formerly communist Eastern Europe, and post-apartheid South Africa. In some cases, domestic elites, educated in elite universities abroad, embraced neoliberalism enthusiastically. Others adopted it only grudgingly because they felt that they had no choice but to swallow the bitter pill of structural adjustment demands that inevitably accompanied much-needed IMF or World Bank loan offers. Although Chicago School economists like Friedman disliked the 1940s Keynesian regulatory framework under which the IMF and World Bank had originally been devised, their neoliberal ideological descendants in the 1990s managed to capture the upper echelons of power in these international economic institutions. With the support of the world's sole remaining superpower, they eagerly exported the 'Washington Consensus' to the rest of the world (see Box 5).

Let us now examine in more detail the workings of these four dimensions of neoliberalism across different countries, regions, and regimes. Its variants sometimes diverge on issues such as the precise role and appropriate size of government or take different positions on policy priorities and prescriptions. But most neoliberals share broadly similar ideological positions regarding the superiority of self-regulating market mechanisms over state intervention in producing sustained economic growth. They also agree on policies promoting individual entrepreneurial growth and productivity. Finally, they are united in their view that maintaining low levels of inflation is more important than achieving full employment. We begin our journey through the landscapes of neoliberalism by exploring its three major waves from the early 1980s to the end of the 2010s.

# Chapter 2
# Three waves of neoliberalism

While neoliberalism in the Anglosphere emerged under the conservative leaderships of US President Ronald Reagan (1981–9) and UK Prime Minister Margaret Thatcher (1979–90) in the 1980s, it continued to blossom throughout the 1990s under centre-left leaders such as President Bill Clinton (1993–2001) and Prime Minister Tony Blair (1997–2007). In this chapter, we refer to these two connected, yet politically distinct, phases as the first two waves of neoliberalism.

Reagan and Thatcher's ideological campaign to put an end to Keynesian-style big government was shared by the conservative Australian Prime Minister Malcolm Fraser (1975–83) and the conservative Canadian Prime Minister Brian Mulroney (1984–93). What distinguished Reagan and Thatcher from many other neoliberals, however, was their unwavering commitment to their respective programmes in the face of formidable opposition from within their own parties. President Reagan, for example, considered not running for re-election if doing so meant having to abandon his tax cut agenda. Similarly, when some conservatives within Thatcher's own Tory Party disagreed with her policies of austerity, she boldly declared, 'You turn if you want to—this Lady is not for turning.' Indeed, the Iron Lady would later elevate the slogan 'There Is No Alternative' (TINA) to the trademark of her neoliberal agenda. While showing a strong commitment to their common ideological cause, Reagan and Thatcher also demonstrated their ability to strike political compromises when necessary. And while Mulroney and Fraser's neoliberal agendas took on a more general and diffuse character, they were no less genuine.

During the Roaring Nineties, a more centrist neoliberal agenda emerged under US President Clinton and UK Prime Minister Tony Blair. Aimed first and foremost at bolstering the wealth of capital markets, their approach came to be known as the 'Third Way'. It was widely seen as a politically viable middle way between the laissez-faire conservatism championed by the Right and the progressive agendas long promoted by the traditional Left. A number of European centre-left leaders such as Dutch Prime Minister Wim Kok, Italian Prime Minister Massimo D'Alema, French Prime Minister Lionel Jospin, and German Chancellor Gerhard Schröder adopted moderate neoliberal agendas that they tailored toward their own national circumstances. Still, they all remained open to moving their neoliberal projects in a conservative direction. In fact, some commentators have suggested that neoliberalism and neoconservatism should be used as interchangeable terms. We maintain, however, that these perspectives are not exactly identical (see Box 6).

## First-wave neoliberalism

Let us begin our historical survey of neoliberalism with an examination of the first wave. By the early 1980s, many of the key members of the UK Treasury who had embraced an economic doctrine known as monetarism had become extremely influential in shaping Thatcher's economic agenda. These included prominent Tories like Alan Budd, Terry Burns, David Laidler, Patrick Minford, and Tim Congdon. Most of them were affiliated with powerful conservative think tanks such as the Centre for Policy Studies (co-founded by Margaret Thatcher), the Institute of Economic Affairs, the Adam Smith Institute, and the Institute of Directors. Influential journalists working for the *Financial Times*,

## Box 6  Neoliberalism or neoconservatism?

Contemporary neoconservatives are not conservative in the classical sense, as defined by 18th-century thinkers like Edmund Burke (1729–97), who expressed a fondness for aristocratic virtues, bemoaned radical social change, disliked republican principles, and distrusted progress and reason. Rather, the neoconservativism of Reagan and Thatcher resembles a muscular liberalism that is often associated with political figures like Theodore Roosevelt, Harry Truman, or Winston Churchill. In general, neoconservatives agree with neoliberals on the importance of free markets, free trade, corporate power, and elite governance. But neoconservatives are much more inclined to combine their hands-off attitude toward big business with intrusive government action for the regulation of the ordinary citizenry in the name of public security and traditional morality. Their appeals to law and order sometimes drown out their concern for individual rights—albeit not for the individual as the building block of society. In foreign affairs, neoconservatives advocate an assertive and expansive use of both economic and military power, ostensibly for the purpose of promoting freedom, free markets, and democracy around the world.

*The Times*, and the *Sunday Times* who were sympathetic to the prime minister's neoliberal agenda included William Rees-Mogg, Samuel Brittan, Bernard Levin, Peter Jay, and Ronald Butt. All of these writers emerged as the chief proponents of Thatcher's monetarist economic policy.

In the United States, influential neoconservatives such as Irving Kristol mobilized CEOs of some of America's wealthiest corporations to support neoliberal research institutes and think tanks such as the American Enterprise Institute, the Cato Institute, and the Heritage Foundation. They worked closely with

Reagan and his staff to promote policies aimed at private-sector-led economic growth. A staunch supporter of neoliberal 'supply-side' economics, the president believed that high taxes were the prime cause of poor economic performance (see Box 7).

Prime Minister Thatcher, by way of contrast, held that the growth of the money supply was the chief culprit of poor economic performance. Though cut from a similar neoliberal cloth, the US

### Box 7 Supply-side (Laffer Curve) economics vs monetarism

Advocated by neoliberal economist Arthur Laffer (1940–), supply-side economics diverges from mainstream neoclassical economic doctrines in its narrow (some might say exclusive) focus on reducing tax rates, causing other policy concerns such as budget deficits to be ignored. Based upon the assumption that long-term economic growth depends primarily on freeing up the amount of capital available for private investment, the so-called Laffer Curve is a graphical illustration of the assumption that when tax rates approach 100 per cent, tax revenue will actually decrease. Proponents of this supply–side economics approach argue that new economic growth realized from additional investment in the private capital markets will automatically generate tax revenue surpluses. Reagan and Republican Party legislators in the US Congress found this form of 'trickle down economics' appealing because it would legitimate their political objective of cutting taxes while continuing to fund popular social entitlement programmes like Social Security and Medicare. However, reality turned out to be different. The income tax cuts that Reagan implemented in his first term resulted in severe revenue shortfalls that had to be offset subsequently by increasing taxes on corporate profits in his second.

*(Continued)*

**Box 7 Continued**

Associated today mostly with the work of Nobel Prize winning economist Milton Friedman, 'monetarism' is an economic doctrine that is based on the premise that the money supply (the amount of money circulating in the economy) is the main factor that, in the short term, determines a given country's GDP, and, in the long term, determines price levels in the market. Accordingly, monetarists believe that governments and central banks should be first and foremost concerned with controlling the growth of the money supply in order to keep inflation in check. Thus, along with fiscal policies such as taxing and spending, monetary policy can be used by governments to influence the performance of the national economy by making adjustments to the interest rates to either increase or decrease the amount of money that is released into the economy. Assuming that free markets tend toward natural equilibriums when left alone, monetarists argue that when governments attempt to manipulate the natural rate of monetary growth—for example, to increase demand during a recession—they will create market distortions leading to economic instability, especially over the long term.

president's and the prime minister's differing views inspired distinct policy agendas. Table 1 illustrates these variations on the neoliberal theme.

## Reaganomics

Immediately upon taking office in 1981, President Ronald Reagan announced his supply-side-oriented Program for Economic Recovery that was based on neoliberal principles, specifically the supply-side ideas espoused by Arthur Laffer (see Illustration 4). The new president entered office eager to implement his plan for combating the toxic mixture of stagflation and high unemployment that the country had inherited from the Carter

**Table 1. Reaganomics and Thatcherism: supply-side and monetarist neoliberalism**

| Executive leader | Core neoliberal beliefs | Secondary beliefs | Core neoliberal policy issue | Secondary policy issue |
|---|---|---|---|---|
| **Reagan** (supply-sider) | Government is inefficient. Government predation leads to poor economic performance. | Monetary and fiscal stability is necessary for economic growth. | Restrict the extent of government predation through minimal taxation. | Create economic stability through deficit reduction and spending restraint. |
| **Thatcher** (monetarist) | Government is inefficient. Monetary and fiscal stability is necessary for economic growth. | Government predation leads to poor economic performance. | Create economic stability through deficit reduction and spending restraint. | Restrict the extent of predation through minimal taxation. |

Adapted from Ravi K. Roy and Arthur T. Denzau, *Fiscal Policy Convergence from Reagan to Blair: The Left Veers Right* (Routledge, 2003), p. 12. This table appears courtesy of Routledge.

4. **Ronald Reagan (1911–2004), 40th President of the United States of America (1981–9).**

years. 'Reaganomics', as it would become known, focused, first and foremost, on reducing marginal tax rates. But the president was no less determined to tackle deficit spending and existing government regulations. The only area in which Reagan pushed strongly for spending increases was military defence, which he insisted was necessary for winning the Cold War against the

Soviet 'Evil Empire' and other 'communist aggressors' around the world.

Although both Reagan and Thatcher saw inflation as an impediment to growth, supply-siders like the US president equated monetarism with a politics of austerity. Believing that the money supply would naturally adjust to market imperatives, Reagan did not share the prime minister's monetarist fear of budget deficits. Lower taxes, he asserted, would increase economic growth, which, in turn, would automatically generate sufficient revenues to cover existing spending for public programmes. Derided by George H. W. Bush and other sceptics in his own party as 'voodoo economics', Reagan's neoliberal approach was ultimately disavowed by his own Budget Director, David Stockman. Stockman, a more traditional conservative, publicly warned that deep tax cuts and increased military spending would make large deficits inevitable and advised the president to curtail funding for popular social programmes. Aware of the political damage such cuts could inflict on his chances for re-election in 1984, Reagan stayed his supply-sider course.

Still, Reagan's long-standing resentment against government growth, represented by large social entitlement programmes such as Medicare and Social Security, paved the way for his endorsement of the historic Gramm–Rudman–Hollings Deficit Reduction Initiative (GRH). Also known as the Balanced Budget and Emergency Control Act, GRH was introduced in 1985 as a comprehensive approach of controlling excessive government spending by the Reagan administration. GRH outlined spending targets that would eliminate the deficit by 1991. Sponsored by Republican Senators Phil Gramm and Warren Rudman as well as Democratic Senator Fritz Hollings, the legislation triggered an intense public debate in the global North over the potential dangers of excessive government deficit spending to the world economy.

Though fiscal policy was a major focus of Reaganomics, regulatory reform was soon to follow. Undertaken as part of Reagan's ideological commitment to New Federalism—a doctrine emphasizing the principles of decentralization and limited government—the president's regulatory reform agenda was inspired by the public choice school of economics (PCS). Operating under the assumption that individual citizens 'vote with their feet', public choice economists argued that local governments maintained close proximity to them and thus were much better positioned to respond to their demands. Moreover, new federalists shared the view of public choice advocates that small governments were less likely to interfere in the self-regulating market.

The imposition of such business rationales on public policy decision-making is an excellent example of neoliberalism functioning as a distinct governmentality. For example, Reagan signed *Executive Order 12291*, which required federal agencies to employ cost–benefit analysis in appraising government regulation proposals. Augmenting these neoliberal governmentalities, the Reagan administration succeeded in diminishing a substantial number of regulatory powers of government organizations like the Environmental Protection Agency (EPA). Indeed, these initiatives are part of the neoliberal modes of governance that emphasize a set of principles associated with new public management we discussed in Chapter 1. While differing definitions and explanations have surfaced over the years, noted public administration scholar Donald Kettl has outlined six core characteristics that appear to be shared in the vast majority of literature related to NPM: productivity, marketization, service, orientation, decentralization, and accountability for results.

Nowhere were NPM and public choice principles more visible than in Reagan's deregulation scheme. Deregulation measures were extended to key industry sectors such as communications, transportation, and banking. For example, the Reagan administration settled a protracted case that directly led to the break-up of the Bell telephone system monopoly into seven separate companies. Perhaps the most controversial initiative of neoliberal Reaganomics was the deregulation of the Savings and Loans industry (S&L) so that they could compete more aggressively with other commercial banks and firms operating in the security markets. The removal of these regulations resulted in a tidal wave of mergers, acquisitions, and leveraged buyouts of some of America's top corporations.

With a deregulated financial market, risky financial instruments such as 'junk bonds' emerged which allowed greedy speculators to snap up struggling businesses with lucrative asset holdings, break them up, and sell off their parts at massive profits. Lured by the promise of quick profits and high returns, many short-sighted speculators overlooked the substantial risks involved in such transactions, creating a legendary stock bubble that lasted from 1984 to the autumn of 1987. In the fall of 1987, a disastrous correction known as Black Monday caused the New York stock market to crash. Only a few years later, rising interest rates put a drastic end to another speculation-driven phenomenon: the burst of the real estate bubble which resulted in the collapse of hundreds of S&Ls. The resulting bailout of S&L-related institutions would end up costing American taxpayers well over $100 billion.

Expanding on some early neoliberal experiments of his predecessor Jimmy Carter, Reagan decided to add to the Airline Deregulation Act of 1978, which diminished the regulatory power of the Civil Aeronautics Board. The historic act, which now allowed competitive bidding for route destinations, resulted in an explosion in the number of airlines and flights and hence a surge in corporate profits. However, no new federal monies were made available to upgrade the nation's outmoded air traffic management infrastructure. When beleaguered air traffic controllers called a national strike to protest these deteriorating work conditions Reagan proceeded to fire 11,000 employees.

One of the most symbolically important neoliberal reforms undertaken by the Reagan administration was its attempt to privatize large portions of federally owned land. Reagan argued that federal land west of the Rocky Mountains would be more effectively managed if it was transferred into private hands. He further reasoned that the revenues generated from the land sales could be used for servicing the public debt. While Reagan's land privatization scheme was relatively short-lived, it came to symbolize the high premium that neoliberalism places on private ownership.

Consistent with Reagan's neoliberal mode of governance, the costs of major social policies ranging from those aimed at the poor—such as Aid to Families with Dependent Children, school lunch programmes, and Medicaid—were increasingly dropped into the lap of the states. The use of a budgetary tool for providing federal funds to states, known as 'block grants', was significantly increased to facilitate the discreet implementation of these reforms. Only major entitlement programmes, such as Social Security and Medicare, continued to be managed and administered by the federal government. But even here, Reagan sought to introduce a lean voucher system in the Medicare programme to boost competition and efficiency. Though it did not produce the results that he expected, the president's high-profile voucher campaign was inspired by the desire to impose neoliberal market principles on the delivery of social services.

Reagan's neoliberal record on free trade is rather thin when compared to the achievements of more mainstream neoliberals such as Bill Clinton and George W. Bush. Often characterized by piecemeal attempts at fine-tuning and adjusting existing trade agreements pertaining to areas such as agricultural commodities and high-technology products, Reagan supported strong protectionist measures against Japanese automobile imports. Reagan's neoliberal supporters, however, argued that these were strategic initiatives employed to force East Asian countries to open their economies to US agricultural exports.

Still, the Reagan administration made some progress in promoting free trade through its involvement on three important agreements. The first was the 1982 GATT negotiations, which sought to promote greater trade liberalization in the agriculture and services sectors. However, the 1982 recession ultimately compelled Reagan to cede to domestic producer demands and opt out of the discussions. The second was the president's active involvement in setting the agenda for a new, comprehensive set of multilateral trade negotiations, known as the Uruguay Round (1986–94). Covering areas from agriculture to intellectual property rights, the negotiations were a major force behind the ensuing free-trade trajectory of the 1990s. These initiatives would collectively inspire the founding of the World Trade Organization (WTO) in 1995, an international economic institution dedicated to the implementation and enforcement of free trade agreements, managing trade disputes, monitoring national trade policies, and providing expertise and training for its members. Finally, the Reagan administration promoted the Free Trade Agreement (FTA) with Canada, which was later expanded to include Mexico. Ultimately, it fell to President Bill Clinton to complete this process in 1993 with the signing of the North American Free Trade Agreement (NAFTA).

## Thatcherism

At the heart of Margaret Thatcher's neoliberal revolution was her deep commitment to enhancing Britain's competitiveness in an increasingly fierce global economy (see Illustration 5). In order to bolster Britain's financial services sector, the prime minister introduced a massive neoliberal transformation that became known as London's 'Big Bang'. Accordingly, Thatcher slashed commission rates and streamlined trading processes through a host of deregulations across the financial industry as well as the

5. Margaret Thatcher (1925–2013), Prime Minister of the
United Kingdom (1979–90).

introduction of a state-of-the-art digital trading system. The deregulations were later credited with fuelling a massive speculative stock bubble, which, in turn, contributed to the worldwide 1987 Black Monday stock market crash.

Inspired by the work of public choice economist William Niskanen, Thatcher sought to reverse the steady trend of increasing taxes on private wealth to finance burgeoning state bureaucracies. But unlike Ronald Reagan, the prime minister was not convinced that lower taxes on their own would be sufficient to revive British industry and generate growth. Rather, the monetarist-minded Iron Lady believed that growing levels of inflation posed the greatest threat to economic growth and stability. Accordingly, she unleashed a comprehensive set of neoliberal reforms aimed at both growing the economy as well as tackling deficit spending head on by imposing a set of fiscal austerity measures that were directed at controlling public expenditures.

Most notably, she adopted what became known as the Medium-Term Financial Strategy, whose principal aim was to shift the focus of economic policy from a short-term tax-and-spend strategy to a longer-term monetary scheme. To the dismay of many of her fellow neoliberals, however, this strategy would ultimately compel her government to raise the value-added (national sales) tax and impose new taxes on North Sea oil revenues in order to reduce deficit spending. Thatcher's broader neoliberal programme called for liberalizing exchange rate controls, reducing regulations on a range of business activities, as well as privatizing a number of key national industries. In order to meet the new employment demands of a dynamic and ever-changing global economy, the prime minister sought to 'flexibilize' her country's labour markets by reducing the power of workers' unions in her country. In spite of some spectacular successes like her famous stand-off with the miners' unions, the Iron Lady was unable to completely dismantle the Europeanist-style union structure that had long existed in the UK. Showing considerable political instincts, she agreed to adopt a compromise in the form of a comprehensive employment retraining scheme aimed at her country's unemployed youth. Relying on a network of service-sector employers, known as Training and Enterprise Councils, this training framework would lay the foundation for Thatcher's famous labour market welfare to work programme—an initiative later extended by Tony's Blair's government in the 1990s.

Although Thatcherism shared Reagan's contempt for big government and large state bureaucracies, it showed little fondness for decentralization and the virtues of local government. Indeed, Thatcher saw local governing authorities as highly inefficient and susceptible to the corrupting influence of political patronage. Accordingly, she abolished the rates, a local tax on private property, and replaced them with the infamous 'poll tax'—or 'community charge'—on a per head basis. However, when confronted with severe criticism from the public and members of her own party, the prime minister was ultimately forced to reverse her position.

Another distinguishing feature of Thatcherism was its neoliberal privatization drive, which was applied to a wide spectrum of industries ranging from telecommunications to manufacturing. Under this initiative, the assets of major firms such as British Aerospace, British Rail, Rolls-Royce Aircraft Engines, British Petroleum, and British Steel would be sold into private hands well below market value with the intent that their new owners would use the equity to modernize these facilities. Instead, they turned around and resold them for windfall profits. Thatcher's privatization scheme also included the sale of vast amounts of public residential units known as council houses. Her government's Housing Act of 1980 would provide long-term tenants with a right to buy option and binding legal rights. But many tenants who could not afford to purchase their rental units in the more appealing areas were relegated to less desirable neighbourhoods, thus shattering high expectations and exacerbating existing disparities between social classes.

Considering state welfare policy to be at the heart of economic inefficiency, the prime minister targeted a variety of policies and programmes. Driven by her relentless quest to cut state expenditures, she sought to overhaul the child benefit provision that provided assistance to all working mothers regardless of means. In the end, however, Thatcher once again cut back on this ambitious neoliberal initiative after realizing that Keynesian social security and child benefit programmes had become engrained in the British social fabric, and hence were politically untouchable.

Operating under the neoliberal idea that the UK's public pension system needed to become more 'responsive' to shifting market conditions, the Iron Lady sought to 'liberate' employee accounts from traditional union pension structures by putting them directly in the hands of individual workers. She also endeavoured to address funding shortages affecting the quality of the National Health Service (NHS) through a set of neoliberal directives that required hospitals to field competitive bids from the private sector. Near the end of the 1980s, the Thatcher government empowered local health authorities with greater administrative discretion and oversight of many health-care services—including the ability to manage costs by issuing private contracts with doctors and hospitals to provide services.

## Second-wave neoliberalism and the Third Way

The second wave of neoliberalism became associated with a new kind of global economic and political cosmopolitanism we call market globalism. In the 1990s, this neoliberal ideology was ultimately embraced by a group of centre-left politicians personified by US President Bill Clinton and UK Prime Minister Tony Blair. Identifying themselves with a politically moderate position known as the Third Way, the two leaders embraced major portions of Reagan and Thatcher's neoliberal agenda while incorporating some socially and culturally progressive agendas associated with the traditional political Left. Hoping to broaden the political appeal of his moderate reforms, Blair argued that his New Labour Party stood for 'social advancement through individual achievement'. Employing this centrist rhetoric, Blair hoped to convey that the pursuit of private-sector-led economic growth could be successfully combined with the government's responsibility to provide a reliable level of social services to all its citizens. At a 1998 policy seminar in Washington, DC, the energetic prime minister announced his intention to create a global network of centre-left parties that would develop a joint policy framework capable of responding to the mounting challenges in the globalizing post-Cold War world.

Similarly, when President Clinton famously announced at his 1996 State of the Union Address that 'the era of big government is over', he was in fact advocating for a more trimmed-down, yet still activist government that would operate more efficiently. Like his UK counterpart, the president was confident that what some neoliberal enthusiasts called super-capitalism or turbo-capitalism could be combined with moderate social welfare provisions and greater corporate responsibility. Moreover, both leaders agreed on the necessity of ridding first-wave neoliberalism of its contradictory neoconservative accretions, especially its hyperpatriotism. Ultimately, they envisioned that their 'purified' product—a socially conscious market globalism—would propel the entire world toward a new golden age of technological progress and prosperity.

Such reformed second-wave neoliberalism had a tremendous impact on the political landscape of the post-communist world, for it represented an attractive model for moderately progressive political forces eager to return to power after more than a decade of Reaganomics and Thatcherism. United in their attempts to liberalize trade relations and integrate national

**6. President Bill Clinton (1993–2001) and UK Prime Minister Tony Blair (1997–2007) in conversation at the 'Roundtable Discussion on the Third Way: Progressive Governance for the 21st Century', 25 April 1999, Washington, DC.**

economies into a single global market, Clinton and Blair would eventually take the credit for the Roaring Nineties—a decade of economic boom but also of increasing levels of social inequality (see Illustration 6).

## Bill Clinton's market globalism

Putting the global integration of national markets at the core of his agenda, President Clinton believed that a sustained expansion of the US economy depended on the economic vitality of the global economy. Heavily influenced by his economic adviser and former World Bank Chief, Joseph Stiglitz, Clinton's market globalism was based on the neoliberal thesis that free trade would bring unprecedented prosperity to both the developed and developing world.

As an ideological project, second-wave neoliberalism emphasized the global integration of markets as a rational process that advanced progress in the world. Indeed, the liberalization of trade and global integration of markets were seen as inevitable and irreversible, almost like some natural force such as the weather or gravity. Second-wave neoliberals like Clinton claimed that markets and consumerist principles are universally applicable because they appeal to all self-interested people regardless of their social context. Not even stark cultural differences should be seen as obstacles in the establishment of a single global free market. This vision of an 'enlightened' form of neoliberalism was designed to convince people that they had to adapt to the rules of the free market if they were to prosper.

Moreover, second-wave neoliberals like Clinton made the *moral* case that a globally expanding, self-regulating market went hand in hand with cosmopolitan principles of universal democracy, freedom, and human rights. In so doing, they aligned themselves with neoliberal institutionalists who emphasized universal ethics and humanitarianism as goods in themselves and rejected realist models that saw military and diplomatic policy as mere tools used for the sake of securing and advancing national power (see Box 8).

Seeing enormous possibilities for mutual growth that would accompany furthering commercial ties with the so-called emerging economies of the global South, Clinton viewed trade as the prime vehicle of his economic liberalism. Exerting his country's influence primarily through the use of soft power—commerce and popular culture—rather than hard power—military coercion—the American president envisioned a digitally connected world of multiplying trade relationships designed to serve America's interests as well as complement old military-based alliances like NATO. This approach corresponded to the traditional liberal claim that commercially interdependent countries were less likely to go to war.

## Box 8 Neoliberal institutionalism

Neoliberal institutionalism is closely associated with the necessity of building liberal institutions—especially in authoritarian and unstable countries—to enhance world trade and global security. It draws its inspiration from two related liberal doctrines: *liberal internationalism* and *economic liberalism*. Liberal internationalism involves using a variety of international policy instruments such as humanitarian aid, diplomacy, and, only when absolutely necessary, military intervention to defend or spread liberal norms and values. One example would be US President Woodrow Wilson's attempt to establish a League of Nations and the United Nations to promote collective security and the rule of law. The idea of a global free-trade regime lies at the core of economic liberalism and is advanced by powerful international economic institutions like the WTO, the IMF, and the World Bank. Contrary to their professed universalist ethics, however, these international economic organizations imposed harsh structural adjustment programmes (SAPs) on less-developed countries in the 1990s and beyond in the name of 'poverty alleviation'.

Clinton's grand strategy included promoting NAFTA and the GATT Uruguay Trade Round negotiations that had been initiated by his Republican presidential predecessors Reagan and Bush I. Finalized in Marrakech, Morocco, in 1994, this new comprehensive trade treaty allowed for a tightening of the neoliberal rules governing the international economic system and established an empowered WTO to replace the GATT. In addition, reduced trade barriers on goods, the liberalization of the service industry, and the protection of intellectual property rights (where the US enjoyed a major comparative advantage) became the cornerstone of the Marrakech Agreement.

But nowhere were Clinton's efforts of exporting the neoliberal Washington Consensus to the rest of the world more visible than in his economic strategy toward the successor states of the former Soviet Union. Based on his strong relationship with the increasingly erratic Russian President Boris Yeltsin, the president managed to flood the newly independent nation with dozens of American economic 'advisers' to direct Russia's economic transition from a state-controlled communist economy to an American-style free-market capitalist one. In addition, Clinton supported the G-7 and the IMF in their drastic recommendations to impose on Russia what came to be known as shock therapy. This neoliberal infusion had been previously employed with mixed results in Poland at the advice of American experts led by Harvard economist Jeffrey Sachs. By the mid-1990s, Sachs had emerged as Yeltsin's chief economic adviser, urging him and his increasingly autocratic inner political circle to persevere with the big bang approach to the economic transition. In exchange for accepting massive loans from the IMF and other forms of economic assistance, the US demanded that Russia lift price controls, privatize nearly 250,000 state-owned companies, and liberalize trade restrictions. Left with no other option, the former superpower conceded.

Toward the end of the 1990s, the dire consequences of the shock therapy in post-communist Russia became obvious in a dramatic widening of economic inequality. A tiny power elite known as the 'oligarchs' reaped almost all of the economic benefits. At the time, however, President Clinton was so convinced of the merits of these second-wave neoliberal reforms—and the eagerness of the Yeltsin government to carry them out—that he was willing to turn a blind eye to the Russian president's increasingly authoritarian actions. Indeed, the Clinton administration looked the other way as Yeltsin dissolved the Russian Parliament, suspended the Constitutional Court, imposed pervasive censorship, and escalated the smouldering conflict in Chechnya into a full-blown war. Affected by the economic blowback of the 1997–8 Asian Financial Crisis,

Russia suffered a sharp decline in its earnings from oil and other resource exports. Foreign investors swiftly withdrew large amounts of investment capital from Russian markets, fuelling inflation, contributing to the meltdown of the country's entire banking system. The Yeltsin government was forced to devalue the rouble and stop payment on $40 billion in rouble bonds. Although the economy eventually recovered from this crisis, the blows to Russian democracy paved the way for a major nationalist-populist backlash under the leadership of the new Russian President Vladimir Putin.

On the domestic front, Clinton's market globalism was introduced in the wake of the 1991 recession that accompanied the S&L crisis and the related budget crisis. The combined effects of these developments led the national deficit to balloon to nearly $300 billion. Shouldering the onerous task of reorganizing budgetary matters, Clinton relied on a cadre of neoliberal advisers with strong ties to Wall Street that included Alice Rivlin, Lloyd Bentsen, Robert Rubin, Lawrence Summers, and Leon Panetta. This group convinced Clinton to commit to a deficit reduction plan of $500 billion over five years in order to keep inflation in check.

Similarly, Clinton's neoliberal ideas on reducing social programmes stemmed from his affiliation with a rising party faction known as the New Democrats, formally organized as the Democratic Leadership Council (DLC). Comprising prominent centrists such as Al Gore, Dave McCurdy, Ed Kilgore, and Joseph Lieberman, these second-wave neoliberals embraced the principles of individual responsibility and accountability in place of the old Left's credo of collective welfare. Indeed, the roots of Clinton's second-wave neoliberal welfare-to-work plan, which jointly promoted labour skill development and public assistance for the unemployed, were firmly planted in Ronald Reagan's first-wave neoliberal Family Support Act of 1988. Clinton maintained, however, that his pro-business policies were intricately interwoven with some progressive social programmes.

In an attempt to demonstrate his support for the working poor, for example, the president supported raising the national minimum wage and the expansion of the Earned Income Tax Credit for lower wage earners.

Rather than offering tax relief to high-income earners as Reagan had done, Clinton's tax cuts were aimed more broadly at bolstering capital gains investments made by homeowners in real property, and securities and stocks, as well as businesses investing in new research and development in high-technology sectors. Consistent with second-wave neoliberal goals of blending market initiatives with social concerns, the administration argued that tax breaks for American venture capitalists and start-up companies would encourage breakthroughs in technology and medical research. Clinton supported a broadly appealing package of tax cuts for America's cutting-edge corporations, such as Hewlett-Packard, Johnson & Johnson, and Microsoft while at the same time increasing tax credits for working families.

But perhaps the most radical neoliberal measures adopted by the Clinton administration related to the further deregulation of the economy. In a historic move, Clinton signed the 1999 Financial Services Modernization Act, which removed long-standing legal divisions between the activities of commercial and investment banks as well as those between insurance companies and brokerage houses. The propensity for moral hazard that might be unleashed with the disappearance of these regulatory safeguards that originated with FDR's New Deal legislation would not become fully apparent until the 2008–9 GFC. Other deregulatory measures paved the way for an avalanche of mergers in the telecommunications industry. Overturning several key regulatory measures adopted previously under the 1992 Cable Act, the 1996 Telecommunication Act allowed local Bell companies to compete in long-distance services and cable TV delivery. Various consumer groups—and even conservative economists—argued against Clinton's claims that this law would lower consumer costs, suggesting instead that it would create local and regional corporate monopolies that would likely result in steep increases in service fees.

By the mid-1990s, the combination of neoliberal fiscal and monetary policies began having a positive effect. The budget deficit declined, and long-term interest rates fell—without weakening the dollar or overheating the economy. As a result, the US attracted new international investment from East Asia. During this period, the stocks of American high-tech companies skyrocketed, and Silicon Valley's computer industry experienced an unprecedented boom. In addition, a number of Asian and Latin American countries adopted fixed exchange rates that were pegged to the stable US dollar, making it more attractive for those nations to buy US bonds and other assets. Flush with cash, Americans began consuming big-ticket items like computers, appliances, automobiles, and real estate.

One should also note, however, the Clinton administration's high-profile efforts in preventing the formation of monopolies and promoting free-market competition. In 2001, the Department of Justice filed a suit alleging that Microsoft—which held a virtual monopoly over desktop computer operating systems—had violated anti-trust laws by replacing Java's Netscape web browser with its own Explorer web browser in all of its Windows 95 software packages. In another high-profile case involving the Intel Corporation, the Federal Trade Commission filed a suit alleging that the company had withheld vital intellectual property, thereby depriving their customers of vital information regarding Intel microprocessors. Both Microsoft and Intel were ultimately given symbolic fines that failed to change a business environment skewed in their favour.

## Tony Blair's Third Way

Promising to put an end to the old politics of 'class warfare', newly elected UK Prime Minister Tony Blair unveiled in 1997 his Third

Way programme that sought to reconcile middle-class concerns with business interests. In order to accomplish his second-wave neoliberal objectives, Blair, like Clinton, was compelled to forge new coalitions and bipartisan networks across the ideological spectrum. Convinced that controlling government growth and expenditures rather than redistributing national wealth was the best means of attaining prosperity, Prime Minister Blair and his supporters sought to expand the political base of their working-class party under the New Labour brand. Blair's modernizers, as they called themselves at the time, readily embraced the basic principles of Clinton's market globalism and sought to build credibility with the business community. Consistent with neoliberal values, the prime minister argued that remaining social inequalities could best be tackled by fundamentally changing the 'paternalistic relationship' between state and society to one based on a 'social partnership' among individuals.

New Labour social policy focused on reconfiguring three basic services: assistance to the unemployed, assistance to the working poor, and reform of the NHS. Accepting Thatcher's argument that more money was not the answer, the New Labour prime minister sought to transform the conventional British welfare system into an American-style, neoliberal workfare programme confusingly known as the New Deal. Unlike FDR's Keynesian-based programme, however, Blair's New Deal would further liberalize work training schemes by replacing Thatcher's Training and Enterprise Council with an even more neoliberal partnership model.

Inspired by Clinton's market globalism and neoliberal institutionalism, Prime Minister Blair emphasized the importance of global cooperation and consensus-building through the intensification of international networks. Distinguishing himself from his Conservative predecessors, he believed that euro membership would pave the way for enormous opportunities for British business and financial markets (see Box 9). Initially, Blair

**Box 9  Maastricht Treaty's 'convergence criteria'**

Here are the treaty's five criteria that national economies had to meet in order to be eligible to join the eurozone:

A nation's annual budget deficit has to be below 3 per cent of GDP.

A nation's public debt has to be less than 60 per cent of GDP (the public debt is the cumulative total of annual budget deficits).

A nation should have an inflation rate within 1.5 per cent of the three EU countries with the lowest rate.

Long-term interest rates must be within 2 per cent of the three lowest interest rates in the EU.

Exchange rates must be kept within moderate fluctuation margins of Europe's exchange-rate mechanism.

*Source*: BBC News, Monday, 30 April 2001.

had great hopes for British participation in the single-currency European Monetary Union. Accordingly, he directed the Treasury to set up several euro forums spearheaded by renowned business leaders. Moreover, the Blair government enacted customs reforms that enabled British firms to pay taxes and issue shares in the new currency. But when the economic performance of the eurozone did not seem to meet his high expectations, Blair showed a growing reluctance to abandon the stable British pound for the seemingly tenuous and fluctuating euro.

In order to bolster his country's global competitiveness, Prime Minister Blair adopted a coherent macroeconomic framework for taxation and spending practices known as the Code for Fiscal Stability. The Code emphasized five principles of prudent fiscal management: transparency, stability, responsibility, fairness, and efficiency, and required the government to outline concrete objectives and rules that had to be developed in consultation with the business community. In accordance with his Third-Way philosophy, Blair established over 300 task forces dedicated to facilitating greater coordination both within and among spending departments, cabinet committees, and business groups.

In one of its first initiatives upon taking office, the Blair government ceded the Bank of England's Monetary Policy Committee full operational independence in setting short-term interest rates while retaining the government's prerogative to set an ambitious inflation target of 2.5 per cent. Seeking to win the confidence of investors, Chancellor of the Exchequer Gordon Brown would eventually grant policy independence to the Bank of England after consulting with US Federal Reserve Chairman Alan Greenspan. The Confederation of British Industry and the British Chambers of Commerce endorsed the move and applauded Blair for openly denouncing union wage bargaining practices when they threatened economic growth.

Blair's second-wave neoliberal reforms also included broadening the tax base as well as cutting both top income and business tax rates. To prevent excessive borrowing for social programmes, Blair adopted what he called the Golden Rule—a measure directing the Treasury to keep public debt from exceeding 40 per cent of the GDP. Asserting that welfare reform could be implemented without increasing public expenditure or raising taxes—except for a one-time 'windfall tax' on privatized utilities—the prime minister endorsed a new welfare-to-work programme modelled on Clinton's workfare model. Given Blair's publicly stated commitment to social justice, this tough neoliberal social policy agenda came as a shock to many of his working-class supporters. The prime minister responded to his critics through his support of Clinton-inspired policies such as the Working Families Tax Credit to aid the working poor and the adoption of a national minimum wage to assist low-income workers.

# Third-wave neoliberalism

In 2009 newly elected US President Barack Obama delivered his Inaugural Address in the throes of the worst economic crisis since the Great Depression of the 1930s. Looking straight into cameras the American leader issued a stern indictment against the reigning economic paradigm of the previous thirty years:

> Nor is the question before us whether the market is a force for good or ill. Its power to generate wealth and expand freedom is unmatched. But this crisis has reminded us that without a watchful eye, the market can spin out of control.

At the time, Obama's words appeared to suggest that the age of neoliberalism might be coming to an end. The young president's strong words appeared to signal the dawn of a new age of controlled capitalism. Indeed, when Obama assumed office many compared him to the New Dealer FDR. At the time of his historic inauguration, Obama was the most popular newly elected American president in over a generation. Admired by the media and the American people alike, Obama commanded an approval rating that exceeded 60 per cent. Moreover, during his initial months in office, Obama's party enjoyed a supermajority in both the US House of Representatives and the Senate. And from 2009 to 2011 his party had total control over the House of Representatives. Indeed, during this pivotal period, Obama was able to get his stimulus package through both houses of Congress successfully and his historic health-care reform programme passed in the Senate. That said, when the new administration assumed office in 2009, it appeared to be well positioned to institute a potent policy mix of social protections for the country's displaced workers as well as impose meaningful Keynesian economic structural reforms that could prevent future crises.

Disappointing many of his progressive political supporters, however, Obama would instead adopt a neoliberal agenda that, in some ways, was even more pronounced than those adopted by his predecessors. It soon became clear that the new president would do his best to cement neoliberal hegemony for years to come. In several important respects, Obama helped fuel the third-wave neoliberal project that has been crystallized in the post-GFC era. First, his neoliberal economic vision was premised on a new kind of thinking about the role of digital technology in creating economic and social value. This 'postmodern' third wave refers to a revamped global capitalism where human agency and decisional authority is increasingly subordinated to big data-driven algorithms. Moreover, artificial intelligence (AI) systems and a robot technology began expanding into the high-skilled job sector such as health care and child welfare.

As we shall discuss further in Chapter 5, Obama's third-wave neoliberal era is still in its infancy. Still, virtual forms of social interaction and the advent of decentralized monetary units and exchange mechanisms such as crypto currencies like Bitcoin (which is not a currency, a commodity, stock, a bond, or a reserve asset) began to transform traditional forms of economic production and social relations during the 2010s. Formal policy-making structures once overseen by sovereign nation states and their agencies began to be replaced by new modes of network governance and private firms. Regulators in this postmodern age have been slow to protect the sensitive information of private citizens such as buying habits, health conditions, and political preferences that are being gathered by digital technology companies and social media platforms like Google, Facebook, and Amazon. Such personal data obtained by questionable methods of data-mining can now be shared with the advertisement sector. In addition, third-wave neoliberalism relies heavily on digital surveillance facilitated by millions of micro-cameras interconnected through a global infrastructure of fibre-optic cables and linked to earth-orbiting satellites.

Obama's presidency (2009–17) marked the rise of third-wave neoliberalism by refusing to impose restrictions on the monopolistic practices of emerging e-commerce firms and neglecting to enforce anti-trust regulations on the tightly knit finance sector in the period following the 2008 GFC. Indeed, oligopoly capitalism flourished across the economy ranging from finance and insurance to 'clean energy' and agriculture. The Obama administration's refusal to enforce anti-monopoly regulations on digital firms such as Amazon, Google, and Facebook (or place restrictions on how they gather, use, and share the personal data they collect) enabled these corporate giants to capture and manipulate the online marketplace to their own advantage.

The Obama administration not only failed to place any meaningful regulatory limits on the incestuous relationships among Wall Street brokerage houses, trading firms, insurance companies, credit-rating agencies, and investment banks, but its pro-industry, post-GFC policy strategy further contributed to the already 'over-financialized' economy. In that vein, the Obama administration extended President George W. Bush's Emergency Economic Stabilization Act of 2008 (EESA) and Troubled Asset Relief Program (TARP) aimed at bailing out financial institutions that had been deemed 'too big to fail'. Moreover, Obama extended government guarantees covering dubious mutual funds and mortgage-backed securities. While the 2010 Dodd–Frank financial reform act imposed new regulations on some of the more egregious Wall Street trading practices as well as adding some consumer protections in the commercial banking sector, it did little to minimize the moral hazards underlying the pernicious practices of investment banks—the main source of the GFC. Not surprisingly, the cadre of neoliberal advisers and Wall Street-connected cabinet members in the Obama White House—including Treasury Secretary Timothy Geithner and former Clinton Treasury Secretary Larry Summers—refused to press for deep and meaningful structural economic reform or advocate for the prosecution of those investment bankers most directly responsible for the widespread fraud behind the GFC.

While his administration oversaw generous bailouts of the financial sector, President Obama appeared indifferent to the plight of the over 10 million people who lost their homes as a result of the crisis. From its inception, his economic recovery plan was designed principally to secure the investments of affluent people and protect corporate wealth; it was less focused on protecting the assets of America's working class. Even the president's historic health-care policy initiative—'Obamacare'— placed the demands of powerful insurance companies and medical firms ahead of the needs of patients and consumers. Initially running on the campaign promise that his administration would implement a comprehensive single-payer scheme, a government-provided option for all, the president settled instead for a complicated, but politically expedient, solution that placed additional tax burdens on already beleaguered middle-class and working families.

Falling revenues and increased welfare expenditures resulting from unemployment associated with the GFC augmented the financial burdens on state governments, which compelled the Obama administration to consider some modest classical Keynesian countercyclical measures. For example, the American Recovery and Reinvestment Act (ARRA) of 2009 was passed to assist states crippled by the crisis through measures that provided increased federal funding for unemployment insurance, food stamps, as well as additional Social Security payments. The lion's share of state support totalling nearly $160 billion, however, was reserved to cover funding gaps in Medicare and education. In addition, the Obama administration increased federal investment in pro-health education and scientific research in 'clean' energy. At the same time, however, the president sought to assure investors who worried about the nation's ballooning budget deficits by imposing a series of austerity measures that involved severe cutbacks in public spending. As a result, states were compelled to address their ever-growing budget shortfalls through additional spending cuts, resulting in layoffs and furloughs of many state employees. This, coupled with having to impose tax increases across the board, resulted in reduced consumer spending. Instead of having the desired effect on the economy that Obama's pro-business supporters propagated, these austerity measures contributed to both the longevity and severity of the recession.

During the Obama years, global capitalism in all advanced countries showed the same neoliberal tendency of eating away at stable, well-paying jobs. Citing the demands of a 'flexible', high-tech global economy increasingly known as the 'gig economy', many companies began adopting strategies to build an 'agile' workforce. But this 'innovative' strategy had a serious downside. Professional labour markets, once staffed with career employees, were increasingly replaced with short-term 'consultant' positions and zero-hour contract workers. Often offering little job security or retirement pensions, these new types of jobs contributed further to the thinning of the established middle class in the global North. While the Obama administration's policies were instrumental in helping to generate the most spectacular economic recovery the nation had ever seen, the wages of millions of Americans continued to stagnate, and secure middle-class jobs diminished. As we discuss in Chapter 5, the third wave of neoliberalism met an unexpected barrier in the form of the national populist backlash to globalization. As we shall see in Chapter 5, this backlash culminated in the 2016 political victories of Donald Trump and the pro-Brexit forces led by Nigel Farage.

# Chapter 3
# Neoliberalism in the Asia-Pacific region

Although the impact of three waves of neoliberalism on Asian countries has been considerable, it should be noted that these market-oriented ideas of liberalization, deregulation, and privatization had to contend throughout these four decades with an opposing dynamic of state interventionism and economic centralism. The bonds between the state and the private sector run especially deep in the Asia-Pacific region.

The 1993 *World Bank Report* praised the economic efforts of eight Asian countries—Japan, the four Asian Tigers (Hong Kong, South Korea, Singapore, and Taiwan), and the three newly industrializing economies of Indonesia, Malaysia, and Thailand—for achieving growth rates double those of the rest of the region, three times those of Latin America and South Asia, and five times those of sub-Saharan Africa. This 'Asian miracle' was attributed to a combination of high rates of private investment, a comprehensive quality-driven industrial growth strategy, and skilled macroeconomic management. Although at times contested, this thriving Asian Development Model seemed to underline that close government–business cooperation within a home-grown cultural framework was the most promising path to rapid economic growth in Asia (see Box 10).

## Box 10  The Asian Development Model

The Asian Development Model rests on cooperative relations among government, business, and labour. Sometimes also referred to as 'corporatism', this model has four basic features:

1. An insulated political-bureaucratic state elite that could focus on long-term economic growth strategies and resist interest-group pressures to adopt short-term economic policies.
2. Government planning agencies facilitate public–private sector cooperation resulting in national 'industrial policies' geared toward upgrading the manufacturing industry and increasing exports.
3. Public investment in education to develop competitive labour markets.
4. Disciplined protection of domestic markets from foreign imports (and domestic control over the capital market).

East Asian governments routinely intervened in their domestic financial markets by channelling money to selected industrial sectors that sustained high levels of productivity. But, as we shall see in this chapter, the Asian Development Model experienced serious challenges in the last decade of the 20th century. Many economists explain the region's sudden turn toward neoliberalism in the 1980s and 1990s with the wave of deregulation initiatives that were adopted in countries across the global North. Western investors were now free to take advantage of lucrative business opportunities that were opening up in the emerging markets. Southeast Asia, in particular, sought to take advantage of these transnational financial flows by lifting regulations on foreign capital. This measure encouraged a flood of speculative foreign investments, which, in turn, led to an unprecedented economic boom in the region. By the late 1990s, however, the investment

## Box 11 The Asian financial crisis

In the 1990s, the governments of Thailand, Indonesia, Malaysia, South Korea, and the Philippines gradually abandoned control over the domestic movement of capital in order to attract foreign direct investment. Intent on creating a stable money environment, they raised domestic interest rates and pegged their national currencies to the US dollar. The ensuing euphoria of international investors translated into soaring stock and real-estate markets all over Southeast Asia. However, by 1997, those investors realized that prices had become inflated much beyond their actual value. They panicked and swiftly withdrew a total of $105 billion from these countries, forcing governments in the region to abandon the dollar peg. Unable to halt the ensuing free fall of their currencies, those governments used up their entire foreign exchange reserves. As liquidity markets dried up, output fell, unemployment increased, and wages plummeted. Foreign banks and creditors reacted by declining new credit applications and refusing to extend existing loans. By late 1997, the entire region found itself in the throes of a financial crisis that threatened to push the global economy into recession. This disastrous result was only narrowly averted by a combination of international bailout packages and the immediate sale of Southeast Asian commercial assets to foreign corporate investors at rock-bottom prices.

spike came to a sudden end with the onset of the East Asian Financial Crisis (see Box 11).

## Japan: state developmentalism meets neoliberalism

As the first industrialized country in East Asia, Japan became a model for the rest of the region. Therefore, let us start our survey of Asian neoliberalism by examining the Japanese developmental state framework and how it adapted to larger neoliberal imperatives. As we noted, in the developmental state model, government plays a key role in facilitating the country's transformation from an import substitution-based economy to an export-led one. In Japan, the Ministry of Finance (MOF) and economic planning agencies such as MITI (Ministry of International Trade and Industry) were instrumental in shaping Japan's successful industrial policy, which contributed to the post-war 'Japanese Economic Miracle'.

Focusing primarily on the export-oriented production of consumer goods, large Japanese industrial groups known as *keiretsu* forged a close alliance with the country's dominant Liberal Democratic Party (LDP). Under this arrangement, the Japanese government helped bolster the global competitiveness of private firms by providing the financial backing of their cutting-edge production strategies as well as supplying them with market forecast data that was being gathered in real time by the country's industrial intelligence agency. With the Japanese government absorbing the 'risks' associated with organizational change and innovation, corporate managers were able to focus on long-term growth and production quality rather than short-term profits. This government–business partnership gave Japanese private firms a competitive advantage over many of their counterparts in the West. The Japanese government encouraged private firms to adopt cutting-edge Total Quality Management (TQM) approaches, first pioneered by American scientist and statistician W. Edwards Deming and Romanian-born American engineer Joseph Juran, to help bolster the country's manufacturing industry. These 'systems'-oriented approaches were introduced as part of a continuous improvement paradigm known as *Kaizan*, associated with Japanese engineer Sheigo Shingo.

By the 1970s, Japan had not only caught up with the West in several key industry sectors such as automobiles and consumer electronics but had surpassed the productivity of the world's most powerful economies. Japan's financial markets remained under the strict control of the MOF, which managed both interest rates and foreign exchange rates. While the US saw private savings slip dramatically during the 1970s, Japan's savings rate reached an impressive 20 per cent—the required level for self-sustaining economic growth. A little more than a decade later, however, the Japanese economy showed signs of severe strain. What had happened?

Rooted in traditional principles akin to economic nationalism, the system provided a partly privatized welfare-state arrangement for the employees of major Japanese firms. Many managers and workers enjoyed lifetime employment—an arrangement that promoted a strong sense of mutual loyalty and promoted organizational stability. A major drawback of this socially conscious system, however, was that firms could not easily adjust to shifting global market conditions. When confronted with dwindling profits and severe capital shortages due to the fledgling dynamics of globalization, Japanese businesses found it extremely difficult to embrace hard-nosed, neoliberal measures such as reducing personnel expenditures by downsizing the workforce. But when an inflated real-estate market and overvalued stock exchange began taking a heavy toll on the Japanese economy, the pressure on the government to consider such measures grew significantly. Further economic shocks ultimately compelled the Japanese government to reassess its conventional economic practices.

A number of reform-minded politicians led by Prime Minister Ryutaro Hashimoto began to experiment with neoliberal measures, in the process altering traditional corporatist government–business relationships in Japan. Under intense public pressure to react to the deteriorating economic situation,

## Box 12 Tokyo's 'Big Bang'

Tokyo's financial system experienced in the mid-1990s a neoliberal transformation similar to that of London's Big Bang ten years earlier. In the previous decade, the volume of shares traded on the Tokyo stock exchange had dropped more than 50 per cent, allowing competing financial markets in Hong Kong and Singapore to pick up a huge share of Japan's business. But Hashimoto's historic deregulation reform package called for the removal of legal barriers prohibiting banks from merging with insurance firms or dealing in securities. The 1996 laws also removed regulations governing brokerage commissions and encouraged foreign investment. Like Thatcher, Hashimoto transformed Tokyo's insulated stock exchange into a vibrant global financial centre.

Hashimoto announced in 1996 a comprehensive reform package engendering a potent mix of neoliberal measures (see Box 12).

In 2001, the Japanese government resorted to extreme monetary measures by slashing interest rates to zero (a policy known as 'quantitative monetary easing') to assist the liquidity needs of banks who were saddled with large amounts of non-performing loans. While these initiatives appeared to ease the economic situation to some extent, they also contributed to deflation, quashing consumer confidence.

Succeeding Hashimoto, the energetic Prime Minister Junichiro Koizumi promised to attack deflation and energize the anaemic Japanese economy with a generous dose of *kozo kaikaku*—the neoliberal restructuring of Japan's national system. In a politically risky manoeuvre, in 2005, Koizumi sought to privatize the Japanese Postal Savings system—the world's largest bank, holding £1.75 trillion in savings. Accused of capitulating to the Western forces of market globalism, the reform-minded prime minister encountered fierce opposition. After an intense battle with some of his own party members, Koizumi was forced to compromise. Koizumi assured his detractors that the large privatization measure would not be finalized until 2017—and could be repealed by any future prime minister. Still, the deflated leader managed to score a few neoliberal victories by reforming the state housing corporation and opening up the mortgage business to private non-bank companies.

In the end, however, the achievements of Junichiro Koizumi's *kozo kaikaku* initiative remained rather modest, especially when measured against second-wave neoliberalism in Britain and the United States. Unlike Clinton, Koizumi failed to reduce the massive national budget deficit because the required cuts to expenditures were not approved by key power blocs in his own LDP and the state bureaucracy. Still, the impact of his neoliberal reforms on Japan's economy is evident in its global integration. Moreover, there is no question that the *kozo kaikaku* reforms introduced new market-based approaches and practices, thus altering Japan's traditional state-managed model.

When Prime Minister Shinzō Abe first assumed power in 2006, his economic agenda appeared to follow in line with the neoliberal trajectory of his predecessors. After returning to power in the years following the GFC, however, Abe's economic strategy, which he dramatically unveiled in 2013 to revive the Japanese fledgling economy, appeared to embrace elements of both traditional Keynesian and neoliberalism. In many respects Abenomics, as it has become widely known, embraces a unique combination of Keynesian and neoliberal policies that share much in common with Japan's other post-GFC prime ministerial governments led by Koizumi (2001–6), Yukio Hatoyama (2009–10), Naoto Kan (2010–11), and Yoshihiko Noda (2011–12).

Abenomics encompasses a set of policies known as the 'three arrows'. The first two consist of large increases in government spending as well as a burst of quantitative easing, which is designed to depress the value of the yen and give a boost to Japan's large export industry. These two arrows point to an economic revitalization strategy designed to make Japan's historically protectionist economy more competitive globally through comprehensive free trade agreements. Indeed, after the protectionist Trump administration defiantly pulled out of the Trans-Pacific Partnership (TPP) in 2017, the remaining eleven participants—including Japan, China, Canada, and Australia—managed to salvage the deal by signing a revised form of the agreement, which has become known as the Comprehensive and Progressive Agreement for Trans-Pacific Partnership. The third arrow refers to Abe's deregulation and liberalization schemes aimed at 'modernizing' Japan's fledgling economic sectors. Areas of principal focus include the country's health services system and its pharmaceutical industry, as well as its agricultural and utility sectors. But it remains to be seen whether Abenomics will succeed in reversing the country's enduring deflation problem which had plagued its stagnant economy for decades.

## China: 'neoliberalism with Chinese characteristics'

Asia's quintessential developmental state model and its neoliberal adaptation also applies to the new regional superpower: China. While the transformation of China's closed economic system was a gradual process, the spread of Western neoliberal ideas, particularly among urban elites, occurred relatively quickly. Today, China is the world's second largest economy, rapidly narrowing the gap with the United States. Some of the country's premier institutions of higher education, such as Beijing's Tsinghua University or Shanghai's Fudan University, offer business courses that are virtually identical to those run by leading Western universities. Indeed, the writings of neoliberal icons such as Milton Friedman, Friedrich Hayek, and James Buchanan have been translated into Chinese and enjoy brisk sales.

Historically speaking, China's capitalist system combines aspects of Maoist socialism and developmentalist-style capitalism. China's capitalist model, which has been aptly described by geographer David Harvey as 'neoliberalism with Chinese characteristics', appears to challenge the Western neoliberal archetype, which characteristically emphasizes individual freedom and promotes open markets. Let us examine in more detail China's protracted journey from a largely closed economic system to its successful version of neoliberal state capitalism.

China's turn toward neoliberalism began in the late 1970s after thirty years of strict economic planning and political centralism presided over by Mao Zedong. Devastating famines followed the forced industrialization project led under Zedong in the 1950s known as the Great Leap Forward. With the regime's crimes against humanity during the purges of the Cultural Revolution in the 1960s still casting a dark shadow a decade later, the pragmatic reorientation of China's economy toward market principles would have been impossible without a fundamental ideological revision of orthodox 'Mao Zedong Thought'. This task fell to the ageing reformist CCP leader Deng Xiaoping, who emerged in the wake of Mao's death in 1976 as the unlikely architect of China's capitalist transformation (see Illustration 7). Moving cautiously but resolutely against Maoist hard liners in his party, Deng spearheaded a nationwide campaign to 'emancipate the mind, unite, and look ahead'. Spouting the politically savvy rhetoric of continuing the Great Leader's communist vision, Dengism represented a genuine search for an alternative model—state-socialism-plus-market, to be evaluated according to our familiar neoliberal criteria of economic efficiency, productivity, and competitiveness. In 1978, the Chinese Communist Party (CCP) endorsed Deng's economic reform package, which marked

7. **Chinese Leader Deng Xiaoping (1904–97).**

the end of Mao's doctrine of 'continual class struggle' in favour of economic construction and modernization. And China never looked back.

In 1984, a small group of innovative Chinese economists met in a secluded bamboo forest retreat in the Zhejiang province free from the influence of conservative party bureaucrats and ideologues to explore fresh ideas and engage in new dialogues about how to move their country toward a modern market economy. The ideas that blossomed from the Moganshan Symposium would inspire China's rise as the neoliberal capitalist economy that we recognize today.

Meanwhile, economic restructuring continued under Deng and was most notably associated with the gradual introduction of market principles into SOEs (state-owned enterprises). As Deng's market reforms picked up steam in the 1980s, SOEs began employing short-term contract workers to cut labour costs. Moreover, firm directors were offered greater operational discretion and even allowed to keep some surplus goods produced above their state-mandated quotas. The prices of products sold on the open market, however, tended to be considerably higher than the official prices set by the state. As a result of these price imbalances, state-owned banks were compelled to subsidize state-mandated produced goods, which quickly depleted China's finances.

In 1993, the CCP leadership began allowing a select number of SOEs to form shareholding companies. In the years that followed, Beijing authorized the privatization of additional state enterprises into joint stock corporations. The next major step in Beijing's privatization scheme was to allow some SOEs to open up to foreign ownership. Large amounts of foreign direct investment began flowing into special enterprise zones (SEZs) that had been created along China's four major coastal cities (see Map 1). These exceptional spaces of neoliberalism had been set up to bolster China's export-based production of consumer goods and served simultaneously as research and development centres to test new innovations. It was within these small areas of neoliberal production that many young Chinese business leaders absorbed new technologies and managerial practices.

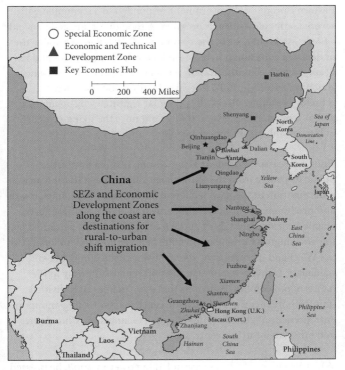

**Map 1. China's Special Enterprise Zones.**

The gradual extension of neoliberal reforms in China over the last three decades did not always proceed smoothly. The 1989 Tiananmen Square massacre of hundreds of pro-democracy protesters brought to the fore the fundamental contradiction at the heart of Chinese society: how can an authoritarian single-party regime extend market reforms without jeopardizing its exclusive hold on political power? Fearful that future popular uprisings might succeed in undermining the authority of the state—as they had done in the Soviet Union and communist

Eastern Europe—the government responded to Tiananmen with severe tactics of political repression. Although it managed to avoid a Soviet-style collapse of the system, the CCP failed to remove the underlying contradiction between its marketization drive and its deeply ingrained authoritarian tendencies. By the time of Deng Xiaoping's death in 1997, the party finally settled on a less repressive compromise: to buy popular legitimacy by means of global economic integration that would raise the living standards of large numbers of Chinese people.

Deng's successor, President Jiang Zemin, further shifted the public discourse from the old socialist values of egalitarianism and redistribution to the new neoliberal objectives of economic growth and profit maximization. At the same time, however, his efforts stopped considerably short of the free-market ideal envisioned by the Washington Consensus. In spite of acceding to membership in the WTO and its support of young business entrepreneurs and managers, China's economic transition remained firmly in the hands of powerful CCP factions that were increasingly divided into the bureaucratic-nationalistic centralists in Beijing and more entrepreneurial globalists in Shanghai, Guangzhou, Chongqing, and other major urban centres.

When President Hu Jintao ascended to power in 2003, he pressed forward with neoliberal reforms, focusing on such critical areas as science and technology, intellectual property rights, and trade policy. At the same time, however, his government remained committed to a state-managed transition to an ever more neoliberal market system. For example, the CCP continued to control the prices and supply of water and power. It also continued to subsidize the inefficient energy sector, which feeds the country's massive manufacturing base.

As we have seen, China's economic framework shares many of the characteristics of the East Asian developmentalist state, including: supporting an insulated state bureaucracy that exerts control over finances and overseeing state planning initiatives; managing an import substitution-based industrialization strategy that paved the way to export-led growth; making heavy investment in education; and maintaining a high domestic savings rate. In other areas, however, it is very different. As we discussed, SOEs have been the focus of Beijing's government-led development strategy and continue to make up the bulk of the Chinese economy. Historically speaking, Beijing lacks the institutional capacity and policy coherence to effectively manage and guide public–private partnerships (PPP)—the cornerstone of East Asian developmental states. Over the last decade, however, Chinese governments have taken successful steps toward an industrial planning institutional framework that bolsters the role played by PPPs in supporting high-tech-led growth. The Ministry of Finance and the National Development and Reform Commission, for example, have been charged with overseeing and improving the coordination among these PPPs.

In many ways, China's neoliberal model is unique among other East Asian countries, which absorbed more Western characteristics. The 1997–8 Asian Financial Crisis exposed deep structural flaws in the Western-led global financial system that China was able largely to avoid. Unlike many of the Southeast Asian economies which followed the prescriptions of the Washington Consensus, China was able to protect itself against the devastating economic fallout associated with short-term speculative investments originating in the West. Despite sharing many of the economic vulnerabilities of numerous Southeast Asian nations, such as distorted markets resulting from government patronage of weak firms, poor regulatory oversight, and substantial holdings of non-performing loans, China was able to avoid most of the serious international economic crises for nearly three decades. Unlike other Asian countries, the Chinese state retained significant control over financial capital flows, maintained moderate levels of short-term external debt, sustained a massive trade surplus, possessed voluminous foreign exchange reserves, and received continuous infusions of FDI. In recent years however, China's ever-growing integration in the global economy has made it increasingly vulnerable to international economic shocks.

As we noted in Chapter 2, the economic profiles of many Western countries in the 1990s shifted almost entirely from manufacturing to financial services. Their overreliance on financial securities, most notably the hyper-expansion of the derivatives market, caused these economies to become over-financialized. China, on the other hand, is not financialized in the same way or to the same extent. For example, China has continued to emphasize value-added production as the foundation of its economic growth model. And while Chinese banks have tended to run corporate debt, most of it remains in the hands of domestic citizens and organizations rather than in those of international investors. Consequently, the Chinese government has retained its prerogative to impose capital controls, and, at times, manipulate its currency value when faced with global economic turbulence and financial volatility.

Furthermore, China's developmental state-led strategy is distinct from the other East Asian economies, which have endeavoured to shift away from cheaply manufactured exports to capital-intensive, high-quality products. China, by way of contrast, seeks to do it all. The world's leading shipbuilder and international superpower now seeks to lead the global market in the areas of artificial intelligence (AI) and software engineering. China also intends to compete in the high-end automobile export market without abandoning its global dominance in low-cost manufacturing. In short, the government's strategy aims at becoming a leading competitor across all economic sectors. However, many Western companies have long complained that they face continuous pressure to share their intellectual property 'voluntarily' with Chinese firms as a condition for receiving access to Asia's largest consumer market. According to some US intelligence experts, Chinese theft of proprietary technology from US defence contractors and other high-tech industries amounts to 'the greatest transfer of wealth in history'.

In spite of China's aggressive military posture in the South China Sea or its construction of vast concentration and 're-education' camps that confine over a million members of the Uyghur ethnic minority in Northwestern China, the Xi Jinping administration seems to favour a combination of traditional neoliberal soft power and conservative hard power approaches. The outcome is 'sharp power', which involves using non-military strategies to influence politicians, policy-makers, academics, and citizens in ways that are consistent with China's national political, economic, and ideological objectives. Sharp power tactics emphasize the use of persuasive ideas, rhetoric, and even propaganda to direct attention away from subject matters that Beijing regards as potentially embarrassing, politically sensitive, or inconvenient. This strategy is often executed through financial contributions to foreign political campaigns or the creation of Confucian Centres at universities around the world. Indeed, many Western intelligence agencies have reported growing Chinese meddling in the political affairs of Australia, New Zealand, Britain, and the USA.

China's use of sharp power is also evident through its censorship and manipulation of digital information at home and abroad. Over the last twenty years, Beijing has been erecting a digital wall around its citizens designed to control access to outside information and foreign viewpoints—especially those critical of China. A new digitally powered social ranking system has moved past its experimental phase, thus dramatically enhancing the CCP's hold on the minds and behaviours of its citizens. Using such tactics, Beijing has not only been successful in limiting access to information and services provided by foreign companies like Facebook and Google, it has given Chinese companies a competitive advantage which has helped them expand their services and products across the globe. Perhaps more alarming, the US Commerce Department has recently claimed that Huawei Technologies Co. Ltd's revolutionary 5G network may be vulnerable to Chinese surveillance.

Consistent with neoliberal international doctrine, China has made great strides to expand its global influence through its support of international development projects that are unrivalled in size and scope. Critical of Western-centric institutions like the IMF that have been slow to address the needs of the developing world, Beijing decided to promote a much bolder set of initiatives directly through regional IFIs such as the Asian Infrastructure Development Bank and the New Development Bank. The country's incredibly ambitious One Belt One Road initiative (OBOR) combines expansionist economic and geopolitical objectives to connect China with Europe, the Middle East, Asia, and Australasia through the construction of a massive infrastructure network of roads, shipping lanes, power plants, and state-of-the art rail systems (see Map 2).

In 2018, OBOR was expanded to include a number of countries in South America and the Caribbean. Promoted as the Project of the Century by the increasingly authoritarian Chinese President Xi Jinping—who managed to secure the ultimate political leadership position for life—OBOR is financed by direct loans totalling nearly $345 billion. In addition, Chinese state-owned commercial banks are expected to contribute over $200 billion and a further $400 billion will come from China's Silk Road Fund. To date, over 150 countries and international organizations have been pulled into the orbit of this monumental effort which, when fully completed, will elevate Chinese influence in the world to an unprecedented level.

While China's evolving neoliberal model has helped create a new elite communist party-allegiant bourgeois class, it also left hundreds of millions behind. Under Beijing's massive urbanization project, for example, untold numbers of Chinese

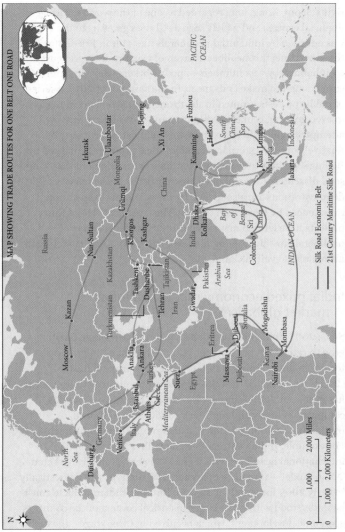

MAP SHOWING TRADE ROUTES FOR ONE BELT ONE ROAD

—— Silk Road Economic Belt
—— 21st Century Maritime Silk Road

**Map 2. The geographical reach of the Chinese One Belt One Road initiative.**

citizens have been dispossessed of land and economic property rights. Hong Kong, long regarded as one of the world's leading financial centres and widely seen as China's gateway to the West, was admired by influential neoliberals like Milton Friedman. At the same time, this neoliberal haven of wealthy entrepreneurs is co-inhabited by vast numbers of poor workers who can barely earn enough to make ends meet. In the summer of 2019, a series of public protests erupted in the former British colony in response to ever-growing economic disparity and increasingly brazen attempts by the CCP to exert greater political control over its relatively open Western legal and political processes. Sparked by Beijing's attempt to secure a favourable extradition bill that would send dissenters to mainland Chinese prisons, these mass demonstrations are also fuelled by the economic desperation experienced by Hong Kong's poor. The large-scale Hong Kong protests have ignited new debates over which version of neoliberalism—the Beijing model or the Hong Kong model—will ultimately prevail in China.

## India: mixed economy meets neoliberal market globalism

Since 2003, India has recorded an impressive average GDP growth rate of 8.8 per cent per year. Manmohan Singh, India's former finance minister (1991–6) and later prime minister (2004–14), presided over the biggest economic growth his country has ever seen. India's success was driven largely by a thriving computer industry and high-tech service sector. Indeed, productivity and innovation had also surged in manufacturing. For example, India's automobile giant, Tata Motors, made international headlines with its fuel-efficient, globally marketed 'Nano model'—a small 'people's car' that went on sale domestically in early 2009 for less than $3,000. But this 'Indian miracle' must be understood within the larger historical context of the country's economic development, which occurred in three stages: the early socialist era (1947–84); the middle period of what economist

Arvind Panagariya has called 'liberalization by stealth' (1984–91); and the current stage of what economist Jagdish Bhagwati has termed 'reform by storm' (1991 to the present).

In the first period, India's economic course was plotted by two dynamic leaders—Jawaharlal Nehru and his daughter Indira Gandhi. The country's first prime minister following independence from British colonial rule in 1947, Nehru chose a democratic-socialist middle way between the capitalist West and the communist Soviet bloc by rejecting both Western liberal economic ideas such as free trade and entrepreneurial individualism and Marxist-Leninist forms of authoritarian collectivism. Promising to safeguard India's national sovereignty, the charismatic prime minister championed a mixed-economy approach, which placed the principal means of production into the hands of the state with the expressed goal of ensuring an equitable distribution of the nation's productive output. Impressed by the ideas of Fabian democratic socialism with which he had become acquainted during his university years at Cambridge, Nehru envisioned an India where economic state planning and democracy were seamlessly reconciled. This socialist framework inspired a series of government-led Five-Year Plans based on a command-and-control model that focused on developing heavy industry and manufacturing. The private sector was subordinated to the state and business licences were only issued for purposes that met the government's planning objectives. Relying on hundreds of state-controlled factories, Nehru's socialist nationalism was bought at the price of economic productivity and growth. Grossly inefficient and largely unresponsive to the people's material needs, only nine of these state-run firms turned a profit. Moreover, the agricultural sector was largely neglected, although 80 per cent of the Indian population lived and worked in rural areas.

When Indira Gandhi came to power in 1966, she actually expanded her father's economic model by nationalizing the largest banks and insurance companies as well as some energy industries. Deeply suspicious of free-market philosophies, she went on to nationalize a number of Indian subsidiaries of powerful TNCs such as Coca-Cola, in the process thwarting foreign direct investment for many years to come. Nationalization of the banking sector, however, had the problematic effect of managers issuing loans on the basis of political patronage rather than according to sound financial considerations. As a result, the number of non-performing loans increased dramatically, ultimately putting India's entire economy in peril.

Succeeding his mother after her assassination in 1984, Prime Minister Rajiv Gandhi cautiously opened the door to a series of mild neoliberal reforms that eased government restrictions on some industries by removing licensing requirements and liberalizing some export regulations. Through tax cuts and the reduction of tariffs on capital goods, Gandhi managed to enhance the convertibility of the rupee, which, in turn, led to a significant increase in trade. Though limited in both their approach and scope, the prime minister's neoliberal reforms delivered an unprecedented, albeit short-lived, spurt of economic growth. But factional struggles within the governing Congress Party over Rajiv Gandhi's neoliberal reform initiatives, accompanied by a major corruption scandal implicating the prime minister himself, brought his efforts to a grinding halt.

And yet, the success of Rajiv Gandhi's market reforms, no matter how limited, marked the end of the long socialist era. Once the neoliberal genie had escaped the bottle, it proved to be difficult to get it back in. In fact, unleashing a potent dynamic of 'neoliberal reform by storm' appeared to be the most attractive option in a country sliding into a full-blown fiscal crisis that had been mounting over the course of the decade. In 1991, India's national debt approached 50 per cent of the GDP. Servicing these loans devoured valuable foreign reserves that had already been reduced to dangerously low levels. To avoid a major default, the Indian government turned to the IMF for a massive $1.8 billion bailout package.

In the midst of this crisis, Narasimha Rao succeeded the assassinated Rajiv Gandhi. The reform-minded prime minister lost no time in appointing the Oxford-trained economist Manmohan Singh finance minister, empowering him to launch a sweeping set of neoliberal reforms that would dramatically alter the country's economic landscape (see Box 13). Viewing the crisis as a historic opportunity to build a new India, Singh argued that it was essential to terminate outmoded commitments to Nehru's economic nationalism. Spouting with gusto French novelist Victor Hugo's line that 'no power on earth can stop an idea whose time has come', the new finance minister promised to realize his neoliberal vision by building on his country's vast and cheap labour markets, its growing number of educated, but unemployed, professionals, and its considerable natural resources.

Convinced by the free-market claims of Western neoliberal market globalists, Singh believed that the adoption of a fiscal austerity

### Box 13  Neoliberal reforms enacted in India since 1991

1. Rescinding state licence requirements for most industries.
2. Cutting the tariff rate on imports.
3. Exchange rate liberalization, increasing the convertibility of the rupee.
4. Courting foreign direct investment by easing restrictions.
5. Removing limits on large corporations to compete in new economic sectors.
6. Privatization of state-owned industries.
7. Lowering the cash reserve requirements.

package and strict monetary policies—in conjunction with sizeable SAPs from the IMF—would unleash India's entrepreneurial potential. In the first half of the 1990s, he cut taxes and simplified the national tax system; slashed tariffs on imports; dispensed with the state's licensing requirements for most industries; corrected India's exchange rate irregularities; privatized key state-run industries; and encouraged foreign direct investment. After he ascended to the prime ministership in May 2004, Singh further expanded and accelerated his neoliberal reforms. Proclaiming that the biggest obstacle to India's success in the global economy was the poor condition of its roads, ports, and energy plants, the freshly minted prime minister pressed for the formation of multiple public–private partnerships to overhaul the country's infrastructure and supply its businesses and villages with cheap and reliable electricity (see Figure A).

To meet his ambitious energy and infrastructure targets, the prime minister committed his country to the development of nuclear power. Acknowledging that India could not develop such capacities on its own, Singh sought assistance from the global community. Reversing Nehru's critical stance toward the United States, Singh accepted George W. Bush's invitation to enter into an expanded economic and political partnership. Recognizing the subcontinent's strategic importance as a potential ally against rising China and global terrorism, the American president became a leading advocate for supplying India with cutting-edge nuclear technology. After a long and arduous struggle with domestic legislators who refused to grant India special exception to the Non-Nuclear Proliferation Agreement, Bush secured Congressional approval in 2008 for the United States–India Nuclear Cooperation Agreement and Non-Proliferation Enhancement Act. Its passage was especially gratifying for Manmohan Singh, who had spearheaded a similarly difficult political campaign to muster support for the treaty in his own country.

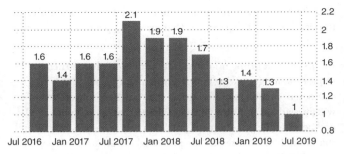

**A. India's GDP growth rate, 2016–19.**

The gross domestic product (GDP) in India expanded 1 per cent in the second quarter of 2019 over the previous quarter. GDP growth rate in India averaged 1.67 per cent from 1996 until 2019, reaching an all-time high of 5.80 per cent in the second quarter of 2009 and a record low of minus 1.8 per cent in the first quarter of 2009. Looking ahead, the Indian GDP growth rate is projected to settle around 1.10 per cent starting in 2020.

In the first decade of the 21st century, some of the positive outcomes of Singh's comprehensive neoliberal reforms were obvious: massive economic growth, exchange rate stability, and substantial increases in foreign direct investment. On the downside, however, his neoliberal reforms had increased the gap between the rich and the poor. The privatization of housing put home ownership out of reach for the majority of ordinary Indians. Moreover, economic growth meant an increase in demand for oil, whose rising price put pressure on India's foreign reserves.

After the elimination of most state licensing requirements in 1991, there was a popular expectation that India's corruption would soon diminish. After all, a highly influential World Bank report claimed that 'policies that lower controls on foreign trade, remove entry barriers for private industry, and privatize state firms in a way that ensures competition—all of these will fight corruption'. Interestingly, India did each of these things: it not only removed entry barriers for private industry but privatized industries and expanded trade. Despite these measures, however, economic liberalization proved to have had almost no effect on the number or the size of corruption scandals that have long plagued the country.

India's current prime minister, Narendra Modi, has earned a reputation for governing effectively through honest and competent members of his bureaucracy. In 2018, the editors of a widely read South Asian journal claimed that his nationalist BJP had become the 'pre-eminent political party of neoliberalism' and that Modi had emerged as 'the preferred candidate of corporate capital'. Following the 2014 general election, a prominent Indian scholar even referred to Modi's sweeping electoral victory as 'India's Thatcher moment'. Despite popular rhetoric, however, Modi's actual policy record scarcely resembles that of a free-market fundamentalist. While the national government has continued to transfer some public utilities into private hands, Modi's neoliberal platform pales in comparison to the comprehensive privatization initiatives undertaken successively by Manmohan Singh and Atal Bihari Vajpayee.

Much like the current US President Donald Trump, Modi seems to have embraced a mix of neoliberal and economic nationalist policies. This is evidenced by Modi's decision to eviscerate nearly sixty bilateral investment treaties (BITs)—an action many pro-marketeers viewed as a direct assault on the foreign investment-friendly policies that were put in place by his neoliberal predecessors. In addition, Modi imposed a series of tariffs on many popular imports, thereby raising them to their highest levels in over thirty years. In what was ultimately deemed a failed attempt to combat the rampant circulation of 'black money', Modi mounted a comprehensive demonetization campaign which resulted in massive cash shortages and disinvestment. Given his policy actions, it would appear that Modi has abandoned much of the neoliberal agenda that was initiated in the early 1990s in favour of one that seems to embrace elements of populism and economic nationalism.

It should be noted, however, that despite Prime Minister Modi's protectionist policies, India's private business community, which had developed under nearly three decades of neoliberal political regimes, has continued to flourish. Indeed, India's largest corporations such as Tata Group (which owns British iconic car company Land Rover) and banking giants like HDFC (and its mortgage company the Housing Development Finance Corporation) have not only survived Modi's demonetization scheme but continue to boast large profits. Another clear testimony to the continuation of some neoliberal dynamics in the national populist Modi era is the fact that over twenty Indian banks remain prominently featured on the 2019 Forbes Global 2000 list.

Consistent with neoliberal views emphasizing the need to expand international cooperation and diplomacy in order to secure global markets, Modi has been working to normalize relations with China—India's long-time military and economic rival. The two economic superpowers appear to be setting aside old tensions in a concerted attempt to forge a united front against American President Trump's punitive tariffs on Chinese and Indian imported goods. Indeed, President Jinping has openly expressed his desire to work with Prime Minister Modi in elevating the relationship between Asia's economic giants to a new level. On the diplomatic front, Jinping was among the first international leaders to congratulate Prime Minister Modi on his sweeping 2019 electoral victory. Marking a new era in Sino-Indian military cooperation, Beijing has since signalled that it intends to begin working with India on developing a new strategic partnership in order to advance their mutual security interests in the Indian Ocean. Jinping's promotion of Luo Zhaohui to vice-minister of foreign affairs reflects the current Chinese president's strong commitment to building a closer alliance with India. Luo Zhaohui, China's former ambassador to India (2016–19), who was instrumental in settling the 2017 Doklam military stand-off, is expected to cement this new partnership. Unfortunately, the recent military stand-off between Indian and Chinese forces along the Sino-Indian border in the summer of 2020 may serve to awaken old hostilities and undermine this new spirit of 'goodwill'.

## Final reflections

This chapter has suggested that neoliberalism in the Asia-Pacific region evolved within highly differentiated political-economic systems that were rooted in a regional developmental state model. Whether the economic turn toward neoliberalism in Asia was driven by imperatives forced upon countries by globalization or was deliberately adopted by market-oriented domestic leaders to suit their own political objectives, we emphasized that this ongoing transformation has not been a uniform process. Indeed, different nations have found unique ways of entering an increasingly globalized marketplace. Once these Asian governments adapted neoliberalism to meet their specific needs, they scarcely hesitated to incorporate suitable portions of an economic nationalist programme recently popularized by influential populist leaders like Donald Trump. Thus, our comparison of neoliberalism's various manifestations in the Asia-Pacific region shatters the myth that the doctrine comes only in its familiar Anglo-American form. Let us now turn to Latin America and Africa to complete our journey around the world.

# Chapter 4
# Neoliberalism in Latin America and Africa

The pro-market ideas espoused by economists belonging to the WC had an enormous influence in shaping neoliberal policies in Latin America and Africa. As we noted in Chapter 1, the IMF and World Bank began in the early 1980s linking loan guarantees for heavily indebted developing countries to a series of neoliberal measures known as 'structural adjustment programmes'. These SAPs put more emphasis on production for export rather than on meeting the needs of national and local markets. They also mandated severe spending cuts—especially for social programmes; imposed sweeping privatization measures; reduced regulation on the activities of transnational corporations; and, in a number of cases, demanded significant currency devaluations. SAPs were often based on perverted interpretations and misapplications of the WC and its policy objectives. The WC's call for 'fiscal discipline', for example, was recast by the World Bank as 'fiscal austerity', leading to the evisceration of many social services upon which millions relied. Moreover, these international development lenders made sure that a large portion of their loans were earmarked for servicing external debts that they had accumulated as a result of the following conditions: deep-seated patterns of social domination left behind by colonialism; misguided development strategies devised by First World aid agencies; the dramatic oil price hikes of the 1970s; the rise of global interest rates in the early 1980s; waning global demand for Third World products;

decreasing importance of domestic markets; ill-considered and wasteful spending on mega-construction projects; and widespread corruption among domestic governing elites.

Let us begin by examining the early spread of the neoliberal model to Latin America in the 1980s and 1990s by focusing on three countries: Chile, Argentina, and Mexico. In the former two cases, the imposition of the WC was preceded by sustained academic attacks on Latin American economic practices. Dominating the region in the 1950s and 1960s, such 'developmentalism' was largely derived from principles of economic nationalism that had been followed by most West European and North American countries in the late 19th and early 20th centuries. Development experts like the Argentine economist Raul Prebisch suggested that economic progress in the region depended on internal industrialization protected by high tariffs and limited trade. These ideas ran counter to development strategies imposed by Western IFIs which were premised on the notion that under-industrialized countries grow their economies by exporting their natural resources to a global market whose prices were controlled by large European and North American corporations. Developmentalist politicians translated these theories into economic policy by supporting the nationalization of key industries such as mining and transportation. As long as private enterprises supported state-directed economic development projects, they were offered public subsidies to build factories and hire workers. The state also placed stringent price controls on food and other basic products as well as making some basic welfare provisions in the area of social services and public education. The execution of these economic objectives was managed through a highly centralized and interventionist government committed to national autonomy.

## Chile and Argentina

As early as the 1950s, members of the Chicago School of Economics were eager to extend their public criticism of the

Keynesian macroeconomic practices of Western democracies to Latin American countries. Strongly opposed to their developmentalist model, Milton Friedman and his colleague Arnold Harberger enlisted the help of the University of Chicago, the US State Department, several large American corporations, and the Ford Foundation to establish neoliberal academic programmes in South America. One of these, the so-called Chile Project, trained hundreds of Chilean economics students—henceforth known in the region as the Chicago Boys—both at the University of Chicago and Santiago's Catholic University according to free-market principles. During the 1960s, such programmes were significantly expanded across the region and their graduates rose to prominent academic and government positions in countries such as Argentina, Uruguay, and Brazil.

On 11 September 1973, General Augusto Pinochet staged a CIA-supported coup that overthrew Chile's democratically elected President Salvador Allende, a strong supporter of the developmentalist school. Immediately after the military's seizure of power, several home-grown Chicago Boys presented Chile's new strongman with a 500-page economic blueprint for the country's economy. Known as The Brick, this document called for extensive and immediate deregulation and privatization measures as well as deep cuts to social spending, the reduction of tariffs, and the lifting of price controls—ostensibly for the purpose of fighting Chile's runaway inflation. Accepting large parts of this programme, Pinochet hastily proceeded to impose these neoliberal policies at breakneck speed while clamping down on his political opponents. While conceding that the general's brutal methods of political repression hardly dovetailed with their libertarian ideals, Friedman and Hayek nonetheless argued that such neoliberal shock treatments ought to be given a fair chance. Indeed, Friedman insisted that the swift implementation of such treatments would return Chile to democracy, freedom, and unprecedented levels of prosperity. But their optimism turned out to be misplaced. Pinochet would hold extensive dictatorial powers for the next two decades, a period marked by frequent disappearances of political dissidents, torture, and other systemic violations of human rights. During his authoritarian rule, Chile's inflation and GDP growth rate stabilized, but the middle and lower classes lost ground as economic inequality increased dramatically. The country's richest 10 per cent benefited the most from the neoliberal reforms as their incomes almost doubled.

The mixed economic and dire political results of the neoliberal revolution that swept the country from the 1970s to the 1990s continue to generate heated discussions among proponents and detractors of the Chicago School over the virtues of these externally imposed free-market reforms. Under the stringent neoliberal programme imposed during Pinochet's regime, Chile's labour markets became at once more tenuous and pliant. In the new century, the new employment imperatives associated with the rise of the digital economy have compelled Chile's labour markets to continue to evolve in a more 'flexibilist' direction. Indeed, the loss of large numbers of jobs coupled with perpetually declining wages has been exacerbating existing economic inequalities and threatening social cohesion across Latin American countries (see Table 2).

As we noted in Chapter 1, growing social anxiety, associated with neoliberal globalization, has recently inspired a wave of right-wing populist sentiment to spread across a number of countries. A number of charismatic right-wing leaders across the world have been exploiting growing class cleavages in order to gain political support for their populist agendas. In Chile, new progressive-leaning social movements have been sprouting up in protest of these right-wing populist regimes and the growing economic uncertainty that fuelled their rise to power. An emerging left-wing alliance known as Frente Amplio, for example, has been able to garner no less than 20 per cent of the popular vote in Chile's most recent election. In late 2019, waves of mass protests were sweeping over Chile. Starting with popular outrage over

**Table 2. The fifteen most unequal nations in the world**

|  | Gini coefficient |
| --- | --- |
| Lesotho | 63.2 (1995) |
| South Africa | 62.5 (2013 EST.) |
| Micronesia, Federated States of | 61.1 (2013 EST.) |
| Haiti | 60.8 (2012) |
| Botswana | 60.5 (2009) |
| Namibia | 59.7 (2010) |
| Zambia | 57.5 (2013) |
| Comoros | 55.9 (2004 EST.) |
| Hong Kong | 53.9 (2016) |
| Guatemala | 53.0 (2014 EST.) |
| Paraguay | 51.7 (2014) |
| Columbia | 51.1 (2015) |
| Papua New Guinea | 50.9 (1996) |
| Panama | 50.7 (2014 EST.) |
| Chile | 50.5 (2013) |

*Note*: The Gini coefficient is a statistical method of income and wealth distribution within a country. A comparatively higher score indicates that wealth and income are more unequally distributed whereas a lower score indicates that they are more evenly distributed.
*Source*: The World Factbook 2020. Washington, DC: Central Intelligence Agency, 2020. https://www.cia.gov/library/publications/resources/the-world-factbook/index.html

increasing subway fares, these demonstrations evolved into massive displays of social discontent. Meanwhile, the number of Chileans aggrieved over increasing economic disparity in their country continued to grow.

Given Chile's relative political stability and economic prosperity in the last years, the size and intensity of these protests has taken experts by surprise. After all, Chile had become known as one of the world's leading incubators for budding community-centred enterprises known as Benefit Businesses, or B Corp Movement.

Focused primarily on creating social value rather than maximizing profits, Benefit Businesses seek to empower workers, reduce inequality, promote social inclusion, and encourage ecological awareness through grass-roots democratic processes. Initiated by a group of young visionaries belonging to today's post-millennial start-up generation, this enlightened entrepreneurial business movement that has been surfacing in the third-wave neoliberal era is inspiring new and open-minded work cultures and lifestyles. Rather than emphasizing neoliberal specification-based measures and nostrums aimed narrowly at maximizing corporate profits, Benefit Businesses have developed innovative ways to operationalize the social welfare value that is created through business practices that contribute to environmental sustainability as well as the improved quality that results from building inclusive organizational cultures.

Still, the country's apparent lack of adjustment to continual economic change has been especially difficult on the poor and thus sparked the recent wave of protests alluded to above. Inequality remains deeply entrenched and the country's middle class is struggling with high prices, low wages, and a privatized retirement system designed along neoliberal lines that condemns many older people to a life below the poverty line. At the same time, the country's political and corporate elite has been involved in a series of corruption and tax-evasion scandals that have deepened a sense of betrayal among ordinary people. Although President Sebastian Pinera has promised to reverse some of the deep neoliberal cuts to Chile's social welfare system, thousands of protesters have refused to call a halt to the massive street demonstrations that have added to the sense of the country spiralling out of control. As we shall see in a moment, it seems that Chile is moving in the same populist direction that Argentina finally turned to in late 2019.

Indeed, the history of Argentina's neoliberal journey shares much in common with Chile. In 1976 a military junta consisting of three generals seized power from the democratically elected government of President Isabel Perón, the widow of Juan Domingo Perón, founder of the national-populist Perónist Party. Maintaining close contacts to Argentina's home-grown Chicago Boys, the ruling generals initiated several neoliberal reforms during their seven-year rule but refused to go as far as privatizing some key industries as Pinochet had done. With regard to political repression, however, they closely followed the Chilean strongmen's strategy of kidnapping and torturing thousands of dissidents they labelled indiscriminately as 'subversives'.

After the collapse of the military dictatorship following the generals' disastrous 1982 Falklands campaign against the United Kingdom, the newly elected President Raul Alfonsin found his country teetering on the verge of economic collapse. Saddled with a huge national debt accumulated by the previous regime and threatened by runaway inflation, Alfonsin faced massive food riots on the streets of Buenos Aires and other larger cities. Moreover, he was pressured by the very foreign creditors who had provided the military leadership with massive loans to repay them as soon as possible. The president responded by signing off on modest deregulation measures aimed at promoting trade and tightening the money supply to combat hyperinflation. Regarded as too mild by neoliberal investors and creditors, these reforms did little to restore the country's economic health. Forced to resign in the throes of the deepening recession, Alfonsin surrendered power to the Perónist party, at the time led by the flamboyant Carlos Saul Menem. Sworn in as Argentina's 48th president in 1989, the former provincial governor promised the electorate that he would never allow the military nor foreign creditors to control the fate of their country.

Thus, most Argentines were shocked when their apparent nationalist-populist incoming president with strong trade union ties refused to revive Latin American developmentalism and instead gave in to the IMF's structural adjustment demands to globalize the country's economy by enacting sweeping neoliberal reforms. Menem proceeded to privatize most publicly owned industries, including the national oil company, the post office, and public utilities like telephone, electricity, and water. Further privatization reforms were undertaken to diminish social security programmes and public pension schemes. The Menem administration also made severe cuts to public spending and liberalized capital controls, thus encouraging a flood of mostly speculative foreign investment.

Determined to stay his neoliberal course despite considerable resistance even within his own party, the president curtailed the power of Perónist national populists by appointing several neoliberal 'Chicago Boys' to important government posts. The most prominent of these appointments, Finance Minister Domingo Cavallo, was entrusted with stabilizing the highly volatile peso. To manage the country's enduring inflation problem, Cavallo established a currency board, which in essence dollarized Argentina's currency. Claiming to have exorcized the demon of hyperinflation for good, Cavallo boasted of having performed the 'Menem Miracle'. For the next few years, the finance minister's prediction seemed to be on the mark as Argentina enjoyed low unemployment rates, monetary stability, and strong foreign investment. Productivity soared and exports reached new heights. For most of the 1990s, the economy grew at a strong annual rate of 6 per cent, even managing to overcome a relatively mild and temporary recession in the wake of the 1995 Mexican peso crisis.

But there was also a serious downside to the high and stable value of the dollar-pegged peso: it had become quite expensive to produce goods inside the country, thus opening up the domestic market to a flood of cheap imports that undermined local industries and wiped out tens of thousands of jobs. Moreover, Argentina's IMF-mediated global integration had made its economy more susceptible to external shocks such as the 1997–8 Asian Crisis, the 1998 crash of the Russian economy, and the currency crisis afflicting Brazil in 1999. As a result of the deteriorating world economy, Argentina's access to capital markets dried up. But this was only half the story. Lacking the political wherewithal to collect taxes being illegally withheld by obstinate regional authorities, Argentina's national government simultaneously faced a massive fiscal crisis. Consequently, the proud South American nation that had been previously celebrated by IMF and World Bank officials as a 'role model' for developing countries was now on the verge of economic collapse.

In January 2002, after months of violent street protests in its major cities, Argentina formally defaulted on its massive public debt of $141 billion. In order to prevent a complete social breakdown, Eduardo Duhalde, the country's fifth president in only two weeks, limited customers' access to their savings deposits and decoupled the peso from the dollar. Within hours, the currency lost a third of its value, robbing ordinary people of the fruits of their labour. 'Argentina is broke, sunk,' the President admitted, 'and the neoliberal model has swept everything away with it.' Economic progress since these dark days has been mixed in Argentina. On the bright side, the country's GDP grew substantially at a rate of nearly 9 per cent per year, thanks to successful debt restructuring and a reduced debt burden, excellent international financial conditions, and expansionary monetary and fiscal policies. On the other hand, however, inflation reached double-digit levels in 2006. President Nestor Kirchner, a self-styled centrist-Perónist, responded to this threat by implementing price and tax agreements with businesses. But his multi-year price freezes on electricity and natural gas rates for residential users only stoked consumption and kept private investment away, leading to restrictions on industrial use and blackouts in 2007.

During their successive terms in office, Nestor Kirchner and his wife Cristina, who succeeded him as president from 2010 to 2015, undertook bold steps to turn Argentina's economy away from neoliberalism toward a rather moderate variant of developmentalism. A vociferous critic of the WC, Cristina

Kirchner worked hard to honour her pledge to nationalize significant portions of Argentina's private pension funds to protect retirees from falling stock and bond prices. Despite moderate political success, the developmentalist reversal of neoliberalism attempted by the Kirchners appeared to be short-lived.

When Argentina's president Mauricio Macri assumed power in 2016, he promised a more 'business-friendly' government that would tackle the country's shrinking economy, falling currency, and rising prices. Thus, the new president promptly imposed one of the most extreme neoliberal policy initiatives that his country had experienced up until that point. Confident that the renewed turn to liberalism would rescue Argentina from the economic turmoil that he associated with his predecessors' 'reckless' public spending and burgeoning government debt on which Argentina had defaulted numerous times, Macri put the sledgehammer to the regulatory state model. In what many experts viewed as a wholesale purge of any remaining elements of the populist programme that had survived from the Perónist era, the President's neoliberal campaign included a potent cocktail of fiscal austerity measures, as well as the evisceration of government subsidies on essential services ranging from electricity and natural gas to transportation and petroleum. In addition, the Macri government made deep cuts in the entire country's public infrastructure budget.

Yet, by the end of his first term in office, Macri's extreme neoliberal measures had failed to deliver the economic boost he promised. Today over 30 per cent of Argentina's population are below or just above the poverty line. Inflation exceeds 50 per cent and unemployment continues to hover around 9 per cent, with youth employment plateauing at much higher levels. Even the neoliberal business elite appears to be dissatisfied. Rather than creating the productivity growth pledged by Macri, Argentina's economy has contracted. Moreover, when the Argentinian peso lost half its value against the American dollar in 2018, the country's central bank was compelled to raise interest rates to 60 per cent—hardly an optimal measure for business growth. These deteriorating economic dynamics compelled the government to seek another massive $57 billion loan from the IMF. Given the country's dire condition, it was not surprising to see Macri lose the 2019 election to his Perónist challenger Alberto Fernandez and his vice-presidential running mate, the former President Cristina Kirchner. Promising to work together with his defeated opponents, Argentina's new president-elect announced that he would seek a new pact with unions and business that would restore protections for labour while at the same time constrain inflation. That said, it remains to be seen if Fernandez's middle way approach, which straddles Macri's extreme neoliberal programme and the Perónist regulatory state, will succeed in the long run.

## Mexico

The conditions under which neoliberalism came to Mexico in the early 1980s were similar to those existing in Argentina. In both cases, market-oriented reforms were preceded by the re-evaluation of developmentalist industrialization strategies involving the erection of extensive trade barriers to protect domestic industries from foreign competition. Characterized by strong government intervention through the development and management of state-owned enterprises, the Mexican version of developmentalism achieved social reforms and class compromise at the price of high inflation and slow economic growth. Like South American countries such as Argentina and Brazil, Mexico compensated for its annual fiscal shortfalls during much of the 1970s and early 1980s by borrowing heavily from foreign commercial banks. In August 1982, Mexico's finance minister, Jesus Silva-Herzog, declared that his country would no longer be able to service its national debt. Mexico's default triggered the 1982 Latin American Debt Crisis, during which most private foreign lenders either reduced or halted new loans to the region.

Relying on massive IMF bailouts to avoid a social catastrophe, Mexican governments in the late 1980s and 1990s were forced to accept the SAPs that were attached to the much-needed capital infusion.

The neoliberal transformation of Mexico occurred in two major stages under two rather different leaders: Presidents Carlos Salinas de Gortari (1988–94) and Ernesto Zedillo Ponce de León (1994–2000). Salinas's fundamental market reform was accompanied by authoritarian political measures, though less severe than those imposed by Pinochet in Chile. The apex of Salinas's neoliberal reform effort was undoubtedly his country's regional economic integration through NAFTA. To implement the trade agreement along with the SAPs prescribed by the WC, the Salinas administration worked closely with an elite group of US-trained neoliberal economists—Mexico's version of the Chicago Boys. Assembling a powerful market-oriented alliance of economists, policy experts, and business leaders representing the country's largest corporations, the Mexican president hoped to attract sizeable foreign direct investments, which he believed to be essential to securing the country's long-term, export-oriented economic future.

However, on 1 January 1994—the day NAFTA came into effect—Mexico's ruling elite unexpectedly found its economic neoliberalism challenged by a popular uprising in the southern state of Chiapas. A left-leaning band of national liberation fighters calling themselves Zapatistas (EZLN), after the agrarian Mexican revolutionary Emiliano Zapata, clashed over the following years with government troops in their ultimately unsuccessful attempt to spark a national revolution. They did manage, however, to draw the world's attention to the impact of neoliberal policies on the poor and indigenous populations in the global South. The Chiapas uprising also resulted in a series of nationwide protests aimed at toppling Salinas's neoliberal government and weakening the power of the Institutional Revolutionary Party (PRI) that had been entrenched for more than six decades. Anti-corruption protesters soon joined this coalition of dissident groups. Political instability and economic uncertainty grew in Mexico with the kidnappings of well-known businessmen and the assassination of the leading PRI presidential candidate, Luis Donaldo Colosio, on 23 March 1994.

Frightened by the deteriorating political situation, investors began withdrawing funds at an alarming rate, thus igniting an economic crisis. Assuming office in these trying times, Salinas's successor, Ernesto Zedillo, attempted to link the newly liberalized economy to a broader democratic political agenda more inclusive of various interest groups. One of the first decisions that the new president had to make was to cut the peso–dollar peg, causing the currency's value to drop by more than 50 per cent in only a few days. In a desperate effort to cement the government's relationship with business and restore investor confidence, Zedillo accepted an IMF bailout package worth nearly $40 billion in exchange for implementing a severe austerity plan that included cutting public spending and raising interest rates. The implementation of these neoliberal measures brought short-term relief to the Mexican economy at the expense of growing social inequality.

Demonstrating his government's commitment to a more open approach to governance, Zedillo initiated negotiations with the Zapatistas and eventually came to an agreement introducing changes to the country's constitution that extended political representation in the nation's legislature to indigenous Mexicans. Promising greater political transparency, Zedillo appointed members of the opposition to key government posts and installed relatively independent judges who, at times, ruled against the government. Finally, the president further engaged in a series of discussions with regional and local politicians in which he signalled his willingness to devolve some of his government's central authority. This new trend of combining neoliberal economic reforms with greater political openness continued under the successive presidencies of Vicente Fox Quesada (whose election ended over seven decades of PRI rule) and Felipe Calderón. Although the latter is especially close to free-market circles in the US, the tight results of the 2006 election in Mexico, which almost resulted in the victory of anti-NAFTA populist candidate Andrés Manuel López Obrador, suggests the electorate's disenchantment with neoliberalism at the time. Indeed, the tenuous popular support for Calderón's neoliberal programme eroded further with the onset of the 2008–9 GFC.

After a decade of relative economic stability but severe social challenges related to endemic corruption and an uptick in organized crime activity, the left-wing populist Andrés Manuel López Obrador was elected president in a landslide. In the spring of 2019, the long-time NAFTA opponent declared that the 'nightmare era of neoliberalism' was finally over. Pledging to reverse key initiatives associated with the ruinous neoliberal models of the past, López Obrador unveiled his 2024 National Development Plan. Emphasizing greater income equality and ensuring social equity for Mexico's most vulnerable populations, the populist president declared that his new development plan would be an inspiration for other countries. Still, when he experienced pushback from disgruntled domestic and global investors, López Obrador swiftly assured his critics that the investments of foreign and international investors would be safe, and his administration would even create conditions that would allow them to get good returns. At the end of his first year in office, the president appeared to embrace a number of other neoliberal tenets as evidenced by his government's use of some fiscal austerity measures to keep inflation in check and its adherence to the much-repeated promise to secure private property rights. However, López Obrador's tentative embrace of 'neoliberalism light', which included new anti-corruption initiatives, reduced social spending strategies, and a commitment to protecting global investments, proved to be unable to halt the sliding momentum of the Mexican economy. In the third quarter of 2019, Mexico officially entered recession territory and the outlook for the country's immediate future appears grim.

## Ghana

Having surveyed the impact of the WC development framework on Latin America, we should not be surprised to encounter the same economic dynamics in Africa as well. Government-led, nationalist developmentalism in the 1950s and 1960s contained an ambitious economic and social agenda beyond the financial capacity of most sub-Saharan African countries. During the next decade, most of these newly independent states turned to both international commercial banks awash in Arab petrodollars as well as public lenders, thereby tripling their debt to $235 billion by the time the Third World Debt Crisis hit in 1982. The stringent SAPs devised by the IMF and World Bank in response to this calamity prompted many critics to attack these policies as 'neocolonial'. No fewer than twenty-nine countries in the global South were forced to adopt the neoliberal model before the decade was over.

During the Roaring Nineties, the familiar neoliberal calls for deregulation, liberalization, and privatization measures were instituted and an export-oriented production strategy was pressed mainly in the areas of monoculture crops and natural resources. The narrowly focused neoliberal strategy resulted in the reduction of domestic food production, thus exposing many African countries to famine, epidemics, and ensuing political instability. Despite Africa's reluctant adoption of free-market imperatives constructed in the global North, the continent's commodities trade fell from 7 per cent of the world's trade in the mid-1970s to less than 0.5 per cent in the 1990s. Instead of economic recovery and repayment of all external debts, the past quarter-century of neoliberalism has seen the lowest rates of economic growth ever recorded in Africa, along with rapidly rising disparities in wealth and well-being.

In the dominant discourse of market globalism, Africa's position in the global economy is often described in terms of exclusion and marginalization. It would hardly be an exaggeration to argue that Africa has almost been written out of the neoliberal globalization 'success story' for its failure to attract private investment, allegedly as a result of 'bad government', 'corruption', 'lawlessness', and 'endemic civil strife'.

As we shall see in the case of Ghana, however, a number of African states have been able to attract substantial external capital, especially for their mineral-extracting industries. According to a report issued by the United Nations Commission on Trade and Development, FDI in Africa had jumped from $2 billion in 1986 to $15 billion in 2003. Ghana's turbulent journey toward neoliberalism was initiated by Jerry Rawlings (see Illustration 8). In 1982, the Air Force Lieutenant led a second, ultimately successful, military coup against President Hilla Limann's national government. Rawlings established a de facto one-party rule, but soon ran into severe economic and social problems. When his country faced a massive foreign reserve crisis in 1983, President Rawlings was compelled to abandon his pro-worker national-populist stance and adopt a series of IMF-imposed conditionalities. Encountering serious resistance from the trade unions and various student movements, Ghana's strongman tightened his authoritarian grip on the political Left to carry out these neoliberal SAPs through what became known as his neoliberal Economic Recovery Programme.

Rawlings sought to transform his country's public sector industries into vibrant private companies which would in turn create thousands of new jobs, raise incomes, and increase the flow of foreign investment. In addition, Rawlings made severe cuts in welfare programmes and slashed food subsidy programmes. Moreover, Rawlings lowered tariffs on imports, removed capital controls, deregulated large banks, and liberalized exchange rates (resulting in the devaluation of Ghana's domestic currency). As in

8. Jeremiah (Jerry) Rawlings (1947–): Ghana's head of state (1979; 1981–93); president of Ghana (1993–2001).

the Latin American countries we examined, the results of these policies were mixed at best. Inflation was substantially reduced from well over 100 per cent in the early 1980s to about 30 per cent by the end of the decade. At the same time, unemployment and the number of people living in poverty increased significantly.

The privatization of state-owned industries mainly served the interests of domestic and international investors who were in the position of acquiring these industries at rock-bottom prices. The principal beneficiaries of currency devaluations were large landowners and foreign investors involved in the production and export of Ghana's cash crops such as cocoa and timber as well as mining in precious metals such as gold. Higher prices for cocoa beans and other cash crops translated into higher profits for large landowning farmers while increasing the burden on small farmers and agricultural workers. Meanwhile urban workers in Ghana suffered as the prices on import goods and export commodities skyrocketed while their wages increased only modestly. The government's removal of capital controls advantaged global investors, foreign creditors, and transnational corporations who were now free to extract their profits with only minimal tax implications. Trade liberalization lifted both import- and export-oriented businesses, particularly those with strong ties to foreign capital investment. Much like Ghana, a number of countries across Africa including Congo, Burundi, and Rwanda are home to precious conductive minerals used in billions of laptops, cell phones, electric vehicles, home appliances, and a variety of high-tech heavy equipment, which in turn allow billions to connect in the postmodern neoliberal e-economy.

Since its abandonment of military rule in 1992, Ghana has reached some significant milestones throughout its ongoing struggle as a multi-party democracy. For most of the 1990s, Ghana enjoyed dramatic increases in foreign investment averaging $133 million a year, and gold production climbed by nearly 40 per cent. During this period the country's financial markets were performing well, though most Ghanaians could not afford to purchase stocks or bonds. But the Ghanaian economy fell into crisis in 1999–2000 when cocoa and gold prices plummeted while the prices for imported petroleum dramatically increased. Once again having to rely on external loans, the government was forced to borrow at exorbitant interest rates, thus pushing up inflation as high as 40 per cent and devaluing the currency by 30 per cent.

Immediately upon entering office in 2008, Ghana's democratically elected President John Kufuor and his New Patriotic Party (NPP) were confronted with a major inflation crisis and the spectre of economic collapse. Faced with few options, Kufuor was compelled to accept a rescue package and partial cancellation of its $5.8 billion foreign debt from the IMF and World Bank that was conditioned upon his government adopting a stringent performance management strategy. The president begrudgingly signed an arrangement with the IMF and World Bank that placed Ghana under the protection of the Heavily Indebted Poor Countries programme (see Box 14). Kufuor justified his decision to Ghana's citizens by claiming that the debt relief offered in exchange for his compliance with the neoliberal directives would allow his government to keep and invest large sums of new revenues reaped from recent petroleum finds back into domestic social welfare programmes.

### Box 14  Heavily Indebted Poor Countries (HIPCs)

HIPCs comprise about forty developing nations with high levels of poverty and indebtedness. They are eligible for special assistance from the IMF and the World Bank, which provide them with debt relief and low-interest loans to reduce external debt burden to sustainable levels. But this form of assistance depends on the ability of national governments to meet a clearly defined range of economic management and performance targets.

The economic strain experienced by Ghana and its people during Kufuor's and his NPP's regime has made the country's protracted transition to a liberal democracy even more challenging. In 2009, Kufuor and his party surrendered power to Rawlings's National Democratic Congress Party (NDCP) now led by John Atta Mills. However, when Mills died in office in 2012, his vice-president, Dramani Mahama (who that same year survived an eight-month trial contesting his election led by Kufuor's New Patriotic Party), would resume a moderate neoliberal agenda aimed at stabilizing the national economy and achieving sustainable levels of growth. Indeed, over the last decade, NDCP leaders have taken credit for helping to create an impressive growth rate of over 6 per cent annually.

After the extremely tight and heated election of 2017, the NPP reassumed power under the leadership of President Nana Addo Dankwa Akufo-Addo. The new president made a name for himself in the 1990s as one of the leaders of Alliance for Change, a civil society organization opposed to Rawlings's neoliberal model and his systematic human rights violations. Within a year of assuming office in 2018, the Akufo-Addo government launched the seven-year Coordinated Programme of Economic and Social Development policies that followed in line with an ambitious forty-year plan to achieve accelerated economic growth and improved quality of life. Based on an aggressive poverty-reduction strategy emphasizing private investment, intensified industrialization, and public–private partnerships, the ambitious programme is clearly rooted in core neoliberal principles. At the same time, however, Akufo-Addo also included some developmentalist state measures such as strengthening social protection and public services, especially in the health and education sectors. Like most countries in the global South, however, Ghana suffers from the long-term effect of centuries of Western colonialism and thus has a long way to go to catch up with the rich countries in the developed world (see Table 3).

**Table 3. Ghana's human development index in comparison (Human Development Report Office 2018)**

| HDI value | Life expectancy at birth (years) | Expected years of schooling | Mean years of schooling | GDP per capita (purchasing power parity US$) |
|---|---|---|---|---|
| 1. Norway (0.953) | 1. Hong Kong (SAR) (84.1) | 1. Australia (22.9) | 1. Germany (14.1) | 1. Qatar ($116.818) |
| 138. Vanuatu (0.603) | 160. South Africa (63.4) | 138. Burundi (11.7) | 123. Tunisia (7.2) | Honduras ($4,215) |
| 139. Lao People's Democratic Republic (0.061) | 161. Mauritania (63.4) | 139. Moldova (Republic of) (11.6) | 124. Egypt (7.2) | Sudan ($4,119) |
| *140. Ghana (0.592)* | *162. Ghana (63.0)* | *140. Ghana (11.6)* | *125. Ghana (7.1)* | *Ghana (**$4,096**)* |
| 141. Equatorial Guinea (0.591) | 163. Liberia (63.0) | 141. Uganda (11.6) | 126. Zambia (7.0) | Micronesia (Federated States of) ($3,843) |
| 142. Kenya (0.590) | 164. Djibouti (62.6) | 142. Bangladesh (11.4) | 127. El Salvador (6.9) | Bangladesh ($3,677) |
| | | 187. South Sudan (4.9) | 183. Burkina Faso (1.5) | |
| 189. Niger (0.354) | 184. Sierra Leone (55.2) | | | 188. Central African Republic ($663) |

*Note*: The Human Development index is used by the United Nations Development Programme as a comprehensive measure of the 'human condition' in accordance with the proposition that 'people are the real wealth of nations'. Indicators such as life expectancy, access to education (measured in terms of years of schooling), and GDP (measured in terms of purchasing power) are ranked and compared across nations.

*Source*: Human development index (HDI) 2018. Human Development Reports. http://hdr.undp.org/en/. Distributed under the terms of the Creative Commons Attribution 3.0 IGO (CC BY 3.0 IGO). https://creativecommons.org/licenses/by/3.0/igo/.

## Final reflections

Our examination of the influence of the WC on Latin America and Africa revealed the existence of similar patterns and outcomes. From the perspective of the IMF or the World Bank, market-oriented reform in this region was needed to produce sustained economic growth and thus lift millions of people out of poverty. To that end, they linked their financial assistance to SAPs anchored in one-size-fits-all economic prescriptions. Even if we were to set aside possible objections to neoliberal doctrine itself, it would seem obvious that anyone seeking structural reforms to make markets work might consider that not all markets 'work' in exactly the same way and according to the same rules. In many instances, the neoliberal remedies applied to Latin America and Africa were microeconomic strategies that failed to account for the unique social, political, and cultural contexts in which they were enforced.

Indeed, years of empirical data collected across the developing world over the past forty years has led many development experts to question how SAPs have been applied (or misapplied) in various countries. While continuing to promote market-oriented growth through the promotion of free trade, foreign direct investment, and privatization, even institutions like the World Bank have begun rethinking their positions on key SAP prescriptions pertaining to the liberalization of capital controls and fiscal austerity. In its *2015 World Development Report*, for example, the World Bank acknowledged the importance of developing cross-cultural understandings between the North and South. Such shared mental models would facilitate the design and implementation of development programmes that are tailored to the specific needs of developing countries in the global South. Drawing inspiration in part from alternative economic approaches developed by Nobel Laureates Douglass C. North and Elinor Ostrom, among others, the *2015 Report* finally acknowledged the dangers of imposing one-size-fits-all neoliberal models across the developing world.

# Chapter 5
# Neoliberalism challenged

As we discussed in Chapters 1 and 2, at the outset of the 21st century, neoliberalism in its various permutations and modifications had successfully spread to most parts of the world. Its powerful advocates in the West had employed the compelling narrative of inevitable market globalization to convince people that the liberalization of trade and minimally regulated markets would result in high economic growth and dramatic improvement in living conditions worldwide. While relying on this potent arsenal of ideological representation, the global spread of neoliberalism required at times the co-option of local elites, often by means of indirect coercion through international economic institutions like the IMF and the World Bank, which insisted on the adoption of SAPs in return for much-needed development loans.

Despite its undeniable achievements, neoliberalism has created both winners and losers in the globalizing economy. As we noted, the uneven distribution of material benefits sparked serious international challenges and crises such as the 1994 uprising of the Mexican Zapatistas against the neoliberal WC, the 1997–8 Asian Financial Crisis, and the severe economic destabilizations in Russia and Brazil in the late 1990s. At the turn of the 21st century, millions of ordinary people around the world took to the streets in

Seattle, Washington, DC, Davos, Melbourne, Manila, Prague, Gothenburg, and other world cities to protest widening global inequalities and sweatshop working conditions they ascribed to the neoliberal trade and development agenda designed by the IMF and WTO. These massive protests gave a clear indication that the neoliberal promise of a single global market delivering inexpensive goods for consumers around the world was not yielding the intended results.

Confronting the market-globalist juggernaut, these alter-globalization protesters successfully coalesced into a transnational global justice movement (GJM). In 2001, the GJM established the World Social Forum in Brazil and other sites in the global South as an annual meeting place. Its anti-neoliberal Charter of Principles culminated in the optimistic slogan that 'another world is possible' (see Box 15).

Second-wave neoliberal governments reacted especially harshly to these challengers on the political Left. Claiming to defend democracy and free markets against chaos, they began to rely more heavily on the coercive powers of the state to keep 'anti-globalizers' in check. In addition, mainstream media pushed the stereotype of Molotov-cocktail-throwing anarchists on often ill-informed TV audiences. These attempts to stabilize the neoliberal model by means of generating fear were increasingly reflected in public discourse.

But the fear factor did not come into full play until the traumatic events of 11 September 2001, when jihadist Islamists attacked what they considered to be the godless and materialistic symbols of the world's most neoliberal society. Just as the global justice movement was organizing demonstrations against the IMF and World Bank, Al-Qaeda terrorists struck their American targets. On that day, nearly 3,000 innocent people from many countries perished in less than two hours, including hundreds of NYC

**Box 15 From the WSF Charter of Principles**

1. The World Social Forum is an open meeting place for reflective thinking, democratic debate of ideas, formulation of proposals, free exchange of experiences, and interlinking for effective action by groups and movements of civil society that are opposed to neoliberalism and to domination of the world by capital and any form of imperialism and are committed to building a planetary society directed toward fruitful relationships among humankind and between it and the Earth...

8. The World Social Forum is a plural, diversified, confessional, nongovernmental, and non-party context that, in a decentralized fashion, interrelates organizations and movements engaged in concrete action at levels from the local to the international to build another world...

13. As a context for interrelations, the World Social Forum seeks to strengthen and create new national and international links among organizations and movements of society that—in both public and private life—will increase the capacity for non-violent social resistance to the process of dehumanization the world is undergoing.

police and firefighters trapped in the collapsing towers of the World Trade Center.

As neoliberal market globalism clashed head-on with global jihadism, President George W. Bush and Prime Minister Tony Blair turned the security crisis afflicting the world into an opportunity for extending the hegemony of neoliberalism on new terms. Thus, in the first years of the 21st century, neoliberal market language merged with a neoconservative security agenda. Countries were told in no uncertain terms to stand with the leader of global neoliberalism—the United States—on the side of 'civilization' against the 'evil forces of terrorism' or face the consequences of their bad choice. To be 'civilized' meant in this context not only to embrace American-style democracy and free markets, but also to refrain from criticizing American foreign policy bent on retaliation. Countries like France, Germany, and Russia, who opposed the 2003 invasion of Iraq, paid a high economic price for their insubordination as the Bush administration simply cut them out of lucrative business contracts for rebuilding Afghanistan and Iraq following the so-called global war on terrorism.

In the nearly two decades following the 9/11 attacks, it became clear that Islamist extremists were not confining their terrorist activities to the USA. Regional jihadist networks like ISIS, Al-Qaeda, Jemaah Islamiya, Boko Haram, Al Shabaab, and Abu Sayyaf regularly targeted civilians and military personnel around the globe. To be sure, these illiberal views are not confined to Islam but can be found in other world religions such as fundamentalist Christian groups like the Army of God and Christian Identity or the Japanese Aum Shinrikyo cult whose leaders demand that religion be given primacy over secular political structures. Still, ISIS and Al-Qaeda are two extremely violent examples of organizations that subscribe to violent forms of religious globalism. Their central ideological imperative— rebuild a unified global *umma* (Islamic community of believers) through global *jihad* (holy war) against 'global unbelief'— resonated with the dynamics of a globalizing world. It held a special appeal for alienated Muslim youths between the ages of 15 and 25 who lived for sustained periods of time in the West, especially in Europe. Jihadist leaders like the late Osama bin Laden consistently denounce neoliberal practices such as the scramble for war-related profits that followed the fall of Saddam Hussein's regime in 2003. Charging the capitalist system led by the USA with seeking to turn the entire world into a fiefdom of major TNCs, bin Laden articulated a religiously inspired critique of US-led neoliberal globalization (see Box 16).

## Box 16 Osama bin Laden's chilling cost–benefit analysis of the 9/11 attacks

Al-Qaeda spent $500,000 on the 11 September attacks, while America lost more than $500 billion, at the lowest estimate, in the event and its aftermath. That makes a million American dollars for every al-Qaeda dollar, by the grace of God Almighty. This is in addition to the fact that it lost an enormous number of jobs—and as for the federal deficit, it made record losses, estimated at over a trillion dollars. Still more serious for America was the fact that the *mujahideen* forced Bush to resort to an emergency budget in order to continue fighting in Afghanistan and Iraq. This shows the success of our plan to bleed America to the point of bankruptcy, with God's will.

## The crises of neoliberalism: from the Global Financial Crisis to the surge of populism

But the most serious challenge to the dominant neoliberal framework occurred in 2008, when the collapse of the American over-valued real-estate market triggered the GFC. The calamity has its roots in the 1980s and 1990s, when three successive neoliberal US governments under Presidents Reagan, Bush I, and Clinton pushed for the significant deregulation of the domestic financial services industry. The most provocative neoliberal deregulation act came in the form of the Clinton administration's 1999 repeal of the Glass–Steagall Act, which was signed into law by President Roosevelt in 1933 to prohibit commercial banks from engaging in investment activities on Wall Street. The reversal of the Glass–Steagall Act immediately resulted in a frenzy of mergers that gave birth to huge financial-services conglomerates eager to plunge into securities ventures in areas that were not necessarily part of their underlying business.

Esoteric financial instruments became extremely popular when new computer-based mathematical models suggested more secure ways of managing the risk involved in buying an asset in the future at a price agreed to in the present (see Box 17). Relying far less on savings deposits, as they once had, even commercial banks borrowed from each other and sold these loans as securities, thus passing the risk on to investors in these securities. Other 'innovative' financial instruments such as hedge funds leveraged with borrowed funds fuelled a variety of speculative activities. Billions of investment dollars flowed into complex 'residential mortgage-backed securities' that promised investors up to a 25 per cent return on equity.

### Box 17 Wall Street's 'innovative investment' toolbox defined

*Derivatives*: A financial asset whose value is derived from that of other assets.

*Securities:* Assets such as stocks and bonds to be traded on a secondary market. Securities derivatives include future contracts, options, and mutual funds.

*Securitization*: The bundling of thousands of loans and mortgages into huge repackaged and revalued portfolios to be sliced up and sold to investors.

*Credit default swaps*: Derivatives allowing buyers to make payments to the seller in order to receive a one-time payoff in case a specified third party defaults on its debt to the seller.

*Hedge funds*: Largely unregulated investment funds open to a limited number of professional and wealthy investors who engage in a broad range of investments including shares, debts, and commodities.

*To hedge*: Attempt to forestall loss on an investment by using such techniques as short selling.

*Short sale*: The sale of securities to a seller who does not own these assets (and thus must borrow against them) but intends to reacquire them at a future date at a lower price. If the price of the security drops, the seller profits due to the difference between the price of the shares sold and the price of the shares bought to pay back the borrowed shares.

*Leverage*: The use of credit to improve investors' speculative purchase power and thus possibly increase the rate of return on their investment.

*Arbitrage*: The simultaneous buying and selling of securities in different markets in order to profit from price differences in these markets.

Assured by neoliberal policies of the US Federal Reserve Bank aimed at keeping interest rates low and credit flowing abundantly, investment banks around the world eventually expanded their search for capital by buying risky *subprime loans* from mortgage brokers who, lured by the promise of big commissions, were accepting applications for housing mortgages with little or no down payment and without credit checks. Increasingly popular in the United States, most of these loans were adjustable-rate mortgages tied to fluctuations of short-term interest rates. Investment banks snapped up these high-risk loans knowing that they could resell these assets—and thus the risk involved—by bundling them into composite securities no longer subject to government regulation. Indeed, one of the most complex of these 'innovative' instruments of securitization—so-called *collateralized debt obligations* (CDOs)—often hid the problematic loans by bundling them together with lower-risk assets and reselling them to unsuspecting investors. Moreover, they were backed by positive credit ratings reports issued by financial reporting giants like Standard and Poor's and Moody's. The high yields flowing from these new securities funds attracted ever growing numbers of investors around the world, thus rapidly globalizing more than US$1 trillion worth of what came to be known as 'toxic assets'.

In mid-2007, however, the financial steamroller finally ran out of fuel when seriously over-valued American real estate markets began to drop and foreclosures shot up dramatically. In 2008, some of the largest and most venerable financial institutions, insurance companies, and government-sponsored underwriters of mortgages such as Lehman Brothers, Bear Stearns, Merrill Lynch, Goldman Sachs, AIG, Citicorp, J. P. Morgan Chase, IndyMac Bank, Morgan Stanley, Fannie Mae, and Freddie Mac—to name but a few—either declared bankruptcy or had to be bailed out by the US taxpayers. Ultimately, both the conservative Bush II and the liberal Obama administrations found common ground in spending hundreds of billions of dollars on distressed mortgage securities, sometimes in return for a government share in the businesses involved.

The UK and most other industrialized countries followed suit with their own multibillion-dollar bailout packages, hoping that such massive injections of capital into ailing financial markets would help prop up financial institutions deemed too big to fail (see Figure B). But one of the major consequences of the failing financial system was that banks trying to rebuild their capital base could hardly afford to keep lending large amounts of money. The flow of global credit froze to a trickle and businesses and individuals who relied on credit found it much more difficult to obtain. This credit shortage, in turn, impacted the profitability of many businesses, forcing them to cut back production and lay off workers. Industrial output declined, and unemployment shot up, as the world's stock markets dropped dramatically (see Figure C).

By 2009, the GFC had turned into what came to be known as the Great Recession. 14.3 trillion dollars, or 33 per cent of the value

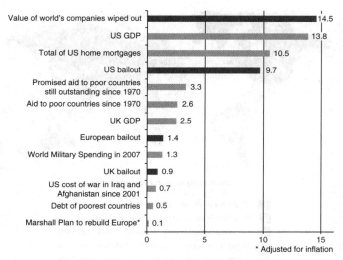

**B. GFC: losses and bailouts for USA and European countries in context.**

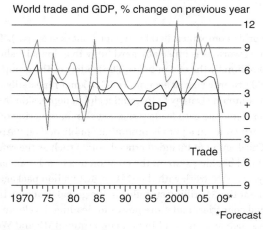

World trade and GDP, % change on previous year

GDP

Trade

1970  75  80  85  90  95  00  05  09*

*Forecast

**C. The collapse of world trade.**

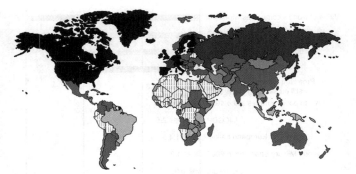

**(2007-2009) WORLD FINANCIAL CRISIS**

■ Countries in official recession (two consecutive quarters)
■ Countries in unofficial recession (one quarter)
■ Countries with economic slowdown of more than 1.0%
■ Countries with economic slowdown of more than 0.5%
□ Countries with economic slowdown of more than 0.1%
▦ Countries with economic acceleration
(Between 2007 and 2008, as estimates of December 2008 by the International Monetary Fund)

**Map 3. Countries falling into recession as a result of the GFC.**

of the world's companies, had been wiped out (see Map 3). The developing world was especially hard hit with a financial shortfall of $700 billion by the end of 2010. The leaders of the group of the world's twenty largest economies (G20) met repeatedly to devise a common strategy to forestall a global depression. After initial tensions, the G20 leaders succeeded in hammering out the general principles in a joint communiqué published on 2 April 2009. The document included crucial points such as the reform of the global banking system; the creation of a new Financial Stability Board to work with the IMF; a $1.1 trillion package to supplement the $5 trillion stimulus to the global economy by individual countries; and more power for leading developing countries such as China and India to determine IMF and World Bank policies.

Neoliberalism

Still, political leaders both on the Left and the Right not only openly questioned the tenets of neoliberalism, but also argued in favour of greater regulatory oversight by national and global institutions. Former Federal Reserve Chairman Alan Greenspan admitted in front of the US Congressional Committee on Oversight and Government Reform that his neoliberal ideology was no longer working. Even prominent conservatives writing for large audiences like *New York Times* columnist David Brooks conceded that free markets were not self-regulating and perfectly efficient, and people were not always good guardians of their own self-interest.

But perhaps the most comprehensive and sophisticated criticism of the neoliberal model came in March 2009 in the form of a 65-page United Nations Conference on Trade and Development (UNCTAD) Report, titled 'The Global Economic Crisis: Systematic Failures and Multilateral Remedies'. The UNCTAD Report emphasized that 'market fundamentalist *laissez-faire*' of the last two decades had dramatically failed the test on real-world application. Financial deregulation had created the build-up of huge financial risks whose unwinding had pushed the global economy into debt deflation that, ultimately, could only be countered by government debt inflation. Moreover, 'blind faith in the efficiency of deregulated financial markets' and the absence of a cooperative financial and monetary system had created an illusion of risk-free profits and licensed profligacy through speculative finance. Finally, the report pointed fingers at the growing role of financial conglomerates on commodities and derivatives, which had led to extreme volatility and the emergence of speculative investment bubbles such as those that developed in the US housing market.

Although most countries gradually pulled out of the Great Recession by the early 2010s, economic growth in many parts of the world remained anaemic and unemployment numbers came down only very slowly. Soon it became clear that the GFC had spawned a severe European Sovereign Debt Crisis (ESDC) and a banking crisis. The rapidly escalating financial turmoil in the eurozone not only threatened the fragile recovery of the global economy, but also came close to bankrupting the birthplace of Western civilization—Greece. It began in 2009 and 2010 when the Greek government announced that it had understated its national budget deficits for years and was running out of funds. With Greece shut out from borrowing in global financial markets, the IMF and European Central Bank (ECB) were forced to put together two massive bailout packages totalling $275 billion in order to avoid the country's financial collapse. But the EU lenders imposed harsh austerity terms in exchange for the loan, which caused further economic hardship and failed to restore economic stability. Greece's economy shrank by a quarter and the national unemployment rate shot up to 25 per cent. This disastrous economic development exacerbated people's resentment of the neoliberal policies of austerity and sharpened the country's political polarization.

In 2015, Greece's left-leaning populist Syriza Party scored a surprising election victory, making its charismatic leader, Alexis Tsipras, the new prime minister. After multiple rejections of a tough bailout package proposed by Germany-led EU lenders and the defeat of a national referendum on the package by 61 per cent of the popular vote, Tsipras was nonetheless forced to bow to growing popular fears that the dire economic situation in the country would become much worse if it did not accede to the humiliating EU bailout package. After heated debates, the Greek parliament approved the debt relief measure and promised to implement its highly contentious conditions, which included tax increases for farmers and major cuts in the public pension system. As a result of Greece's capitulation, the EU creditors offered an even larger multi-billion loan over three years, albeit with similar austerity conditions attached, which, in turn, caused continuous political upheaval and unrest in the troubled country.

For the entire decade of the 2010s, Greece had to rely on international creditors to keep its finances afloat, and tens of thousands of young people left the country in search of greater economic opportunities. While the Greek economy recorded a modest turnaround reflected in an annual growth rate of about 2 per cent from 2017 to 2019, most ordinary citizens complained that they were not feeling any significant improvement in their lives. This enduring popular dissatisfaction corresponded to the country's stubbornly high unemployment rate of 18 per cent as late as 2019. As a result of these enduring economic woes, the Syriza Party lost the July 2019 national election to the centre-right Democracy Party in a landslide. The new prime minister, Kyriakos Mitsotakis, a Harvard-educated lawyer, promised to return the country to economic health as well as tightening immigration restrictions.

But Greece was only one among numerous nations that experienced major market declines in the current of global economic instability and volatility. The most surprising development occurred in early 2016 in the People's Republic of China—a country many observers consider the bastion of economic health accounting for over 9 per cent of world economic activity—when its stock markets went into free fall. The Shanghai Composite and the Shenzhen Composite lost 5.3 per cent and 6.6 per cent, respectively, in less than a week. The turmoil in the Chinese markets caused equally sharp declines in stock exchanges around the world. This ominous 2016 slowdown in the Chinese economy coincided with the election of a protectionist American president seemingly eager to put an end to the long era of neoliberalism.

## The challenge of economic nationalism and national populism

Reacting to rising economic and cultural tensions in a globalizing world, nationalist forces on the political Right were also gathering strength in the 2010s. Castigating market globalism for the breakdown of community and traditional ways of life, they also bemoaned the displacement of small farmers and increased levels of immigration in their countries. They also denounced free trade, the increasing power of global investors, and the outsourcing of domestic manufacturing jobs as 'unpatriotic' practices that had contributed to falling living standards and moral decline. In the global South, too, national populists blamed neoliberal globalization and the expansion of American power for economic decline and cultural decay.

In short, the dire economic consequences of the GFC and the ESDC—combined with the perceived threat to traditional cultural identities posed by the enhanced global migration flows in the mid-2010s—caused a profound shift away from the neoliberal vision of a globally integrated world. Ordinary people's belief in the claims of neoliberal globalism gave way to widespread fears that the great experiment of transcending the nation state had spiralled out of control and needed to be curbed. Accusing 'cosmopolitan elites' of cheating the toiling masses, authoritarian politicians soon capitalized on this popular discontent by promising 'the forgotten people' a return to national control.

The full extent of people's anger and resentment was reflected in the unexpected 2016 victory of the pro-Brexit forces in the UK and the stunning election of Donald J. Trump in the United States a few months later. Indeed, the growing power of right-wing national populism—and the crucial role played by the digital social media in its meteoric rise—prompted influential pundits to speak of a populist explosion (see Box 18).

Indeed, the illiberal and authoritarian leanings of national populism stand in stark contrast to the pluralist and inclusive values of liberal democracy. Yet, populism has been successful in both liberal democracies and authoritarian countries such as Boris Johnson's United Kingdom, Victor Órban's Hungary, Vladimir Putin's Russia, Jair Bolsonaro's Brazil, Norbert Hofer's Austria, Marine Le Pen's France, Matteo Salvini's Italy, Jarosław

## Box 18 What is national populism?

The French philosopher Pierre-André Taguieff (1946–) coined the term *national populism* in 1984 in reference to the political discourse of Jean-Marie Le Pen and his right-wing French political party, Front National, renamed in 2018 under the leadership of his daughter Marine Le Pen as Rassemblement National. National populists imagine a mythical national unity based on an essentialized identity linking ethnicity/race and culture. They claim to defend and protect the pure 'common people' against the treachery of 'corrupt elites' and 'parasitical' political institutions. Privileging a direct relationship between the leader and the people, national populists often combine working-class values of the Left with anti-immigrant views of the Right. Over the years, a growing number of populism scholars have adopted 'national populism' as an umbrella term for a range of right-wing variants linked to different geographic regions in the world.

Kaczyński's Poland, Scott Morrison's Australia, Iván D[  ] Colombia, Rodrigo Duterte's Philippines, and, of course, [  ] nald Trump's United States of America (see Figure D).

But this populist surge did not stop in 2016. Over the last few years, national populists managed to consolidate their gains, most recently in the 2019 European Parliamentary Elections. Their parties and candidates vaulted to the top spot not only in their previous strongholds of Hungary and Poland, but also in large, traditionally centrist, countries such as France and Italy. But the biggest surprise occurred in the UK where Nigel Farage's newly formed Brexit Party came in first with an astonishing 32 per cent of the vote. A few months later, the hard-line, pro-Brexit Tory politician Boris Johnson ascended to the prime ministership and succeeded in officially dissolving the UK's membership of the EU as of 31 January 2020.

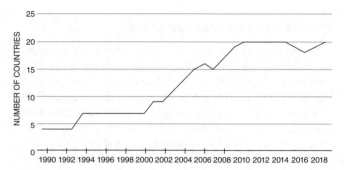

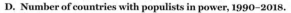

**D. Number of countries with populists in power, 1990–2018.**

## Trump's nationalist neoliberalism

In order to get a better sense of the nature of national populism's challenge to neoliberalism, let us return to our opening scene in Chapter 1 and examine the mixed ideological and policy framework of Trumpism. While our discussion will show that the US president's approach does project some major claims that run counter to the dominant economic order of the last three decades, it also promotes some familiar neoliberal arrangements. Let's begin our analysis by focusing on the clearly anti-neoliberal portions of Trumpism.

An analysis of key speeches given by Donald Trump during his 2016 presidential campaign as well as major public addresses delivered during the first three years of his presidential term (2017–19) reveal his strong antipathy for neoliberal globalism in favour of economic nationalism. This doctrine espouses that the economy should be designed in ways that, first and foremost, serve narrow national interests. In the American context, economic nationalism was first supported by 19th-century Republican Party politicians who sought to protect the country's infant industries from foreign competition, especially from England's cheaper imports. By the 1880s, the GOP had become *the* American party of protectionism and state interventionism in the economy.

Out of favour for most of the 20th century, this doctrine made an unexpected return to popularity in the new century through the efforts of Trump's senior adviser Stephen K. Bannon, who, in turn, was deeply influenced by two nationalist conservatives, Patrick Buchanan and Ross Perot (see Box 19). In the 1990s, the latter had challenged the neoliberal conventional wisdom of the GOP and launched unsuccessful presidential campaigns as candidates of the

**Box 19   Key principles of America First economic nationalism as advocated by Steve Bannon and adopted by Donald Trump**

1. America is a national *community* held together by religious, civic, and cultural bonds—not merely an abstract *economy* feeding into global capitalism.
2. The USA needs to be self-sufficient and maintain complete sovereignty over its economy and production capacity.
3. Imposition of stricter border control by the USA on goods, services, capital, and people for the alleged economic welfare and security of the American people.
4. In particular, restrict both illegal immigration and immigration of low-skilled labourers that push downward domestic wages.
5. Protection of American industries and workers from the influx of low-cost foreign goods.
6. Trade is a zero-sum game: impose tariffs to make American-made goods more competitive to domestic consumers and boost internal production and trade.
7. Support public financing of large infrastructure development, reindustrialization, and job creation for national workers.
8. Convince American consumers to prioritize national products as an investment in their economic prosperity.

short-lived Reform Party. To give his economic position a more recognizable label, Bannon revived the America First slogan used in the 1940s by a small isolationist political group in the US led by the patriotic aviator-turned-Nazi sympathizer, Charles Lindbergh.

Heavily indebted to Bannon's conceptual framework, Trumpism justifies economic nationalism by arguing that it protects ordinary people from the ravages of global capitalism. To that end, it employs national populist core concepts identified in Box 18. Accused of undermining the will of the people with the help of the corporate media, these economic, political, and cultural members of the 'establishment' are said to advance their morally corrupt practices of 'selling out the wealth of our nation generated by working people and filling their own pockets'. But Trumpism also links the meaning of 'elites' to the spectre of 'globalist enemies' working against the interests of the country. While some of these are explicitly identified as domestic neoliberal actors such as 'Wall Street bankers' or 'Washington politicians', others are characterized as 'foreign agents'. These include both powerful individuals such as George Soros and other members of the 'international financial elite' as well as entire countries like China, Mexico, and Japan, which are denounced for the alleged misdeeds of 'subsidizing their goods', 'devaluing their currencies', 'violating their agreements', and for 'sending rapists, drug dealers, and other criminals into America'.

For this reason, Trump bashes neoliberal globalism as a set of misguided public policies and a 'hateful foreign ideology' devised by members of 'the global power structure' who 'plot in secret to destroy America'. Neoliberals serve the larger material process of globalization—defined by Trump as an elite-engineered project of abolishing the nation state and creating an international system that functions 'to the detriment of the American worker and the American economy'. Finally, Trump also associates neoliberal economics with an attitude of multiculturalism culminating in the 'complete and total disasters' of immigration, crime, and terrorism that are 'destroying our nation'. Immigration, in particular, receives ample treatment in the form of vigorous denunciations of the neoliberal establishment's 'globalist policies of open borders' that are alleged to endanger the safety and security of the American people.

The realization of Trump's central campaign slogan to 'make America great again' requires the denunciation of major neoliberal tenets. Indeed, nowhere have the anti-neoliberal tendencies in Trumpism been more visible than in its rejection of the post-war liberal trade policies embraced by Republicans and Democrats alike. Trump's challenge to long-standing trade practices between the USA and China represents the most spectacular illustration of his illiberal tendencies. The world's leading manufacturer in the 2010s, China accounts for roughly 13 per cent of global merchandise exports whereas the USA, the world's most voracious consumer, owned about 13 per cent of global merchandise imports. In 2018, referring to this trade imbalance as the 'greatest theft in the history of the world—committed by China', President Trump fired the opening shot in what threatened to become a full-blown trade war by announcing a 10 per cent tariff on $200 billion worth of Chinese goods. In 2019, his administration slapped additional tariffs of up to 25 per cent on $250 billion worth of Chinese products and threatened to levy further tariffs worth $325 billion. It did not take long for China to impose retaliatory tariffs of up to 25 per cent on $110 billion worth of US goods, in the process doubling duties on American agricultural and fish products from an average of 21 per cent to 42 per cent. In addition, President Xi Jinping threatened to implement punitive qualitative measures that would negatively affect US businesses operating in China. Although the Trump administration struck a preliminary trade deal with China on 15 January 2020, the US president refused to cut back all new tariffs, arguing that the deal was only a first step toward a possible comprehensive agreement in the future.

But Trump's trade wars outside the agreed-upon WTO framework were not reserved for China alone. He also targeted America's historically most reliable trading partners, Mexico, Canada, Japan, and the EU. As of early 2020, the smouldering trade conflict, together with the massive coronavirus outbreak in China, has raised fears of a global economic slowdown, thus signalling the continuation of a climate of global financial volatility that has existed since the 2008 GFC. Even the so-called economic boom in the USA under the Trump administration that saw a significant rise of stock markets and a low unemployment rate of 3.6 per cent in 2019, has been built upon low-paying jobs in the service industry and other precarious and part-time jobs that have kept wages stagnant for nearly three decades. In the post-Brexit environment in the UK, stagnant economic conditions have not improved. The country's annual rate of productivity growth averaged a dismal 0.4 per cent throughout the entire decade of the 2010s, and inflation-adjusted wages are down sharply.

Ironically, of course, the brand name 'Trump' appears to be a poor fit with the doctrine of economic nationalism. After all, it stands for a neoliberal globalism clearly visible in the US president's network of hotels (and other businesses) from Honolulu to Rio de Janeiro. While insisting that making America great again required a shift from corporate globalism and free trade to economic nationalism and protectionism, Trump's personal business activities went in the opposite direction. Similarly, his desire to build a 'beautiful wall' along the 1,989-mile US–Mexican border to keep undocumented immigrants out stands in stark contrast to his lucrative business practices of employing them.

This obvious contradiction reveals the messy mix of national populism and free-market neoliberalism that characterizes Trumpism. His vehement rejection of globalism notwithstanding, the 45th American president spearheaded impressive legislative achievements that contain a significant portion of the three-wave neoliberal agenda presented in this book. Perhaps the two most relevant neoliberal policy successes are the 2017 Tax Cuts and Jobs Act (TCJA) and the 2018 Economic Growth, Regulatory Relief and Consumer Protection Act (ERCA).

TCJA lowered the rate of most individual income tax rates, including the top marginal rate from 39.6 per cent to 38 per cent. It also increased the standard deduction and family tax credits, while limiting deductions for state and local taxes as well as mortgage interest. Most importantly, however, the new law lowered corporate tax rates from 35 per cent to 21 per cent—a significant reduction that led to record levels of corporate profits and a short-term growth of business investments while increasing social inequality and wealth differentials among the general population.

ERCA opened the gate to the biggest rollback of bank regulations since the GFC. Dismantling the safety and regulatory measures put in place by the Obama administration's 2010 Dodd–Frank bill aimed at Wall Street reform and consumer protection, the new measure eased restrictions by raising the threshold to $250 billion from $50 billion under which banks are deemed too important to the financial system to fail. Those institutions also would not have to undergo so-called 'stress tests' or submit 'living wills'—safety valves designed to forestall financial disaster. Finally, ERCA eased mortgage loan data reporting requirements for the overwhelming majority of commercial banks.

However, a good part of Trump's neoliberal agenda was not delivered through new legislation, but by a flood of Executive Orders (EOs) issued by the incoming president within days of his inauguration. US chief executives issue EOs to direct officers and agencies of the executive branch in the management of the operations within the federal government itself. At the end of his first six months in office, Trump announced the elimination of hundreds of existing regulations on industry and business—most of those as a result of EOs. Of the nearly 130 EOs signed by the president at the end of his third year in office (2019), more than half directly or indirectly advanced such central neoliberal norms and agendas as economic deregulation, privatization, downsizing government, weakening organized labour, and the reduction of public spending on social services (see Table 4).

In fact, one could even argue that some of Trump's seemingly protectionist trade measures amounted to little more than rhetorical nationalist wolves in neoliberal sheep's clothing. For example, his withdrawal from the TPP in 2017—a far-reaching trade agreement which would have established the largest free-trade bloc in the world—did not prevent his administration from offering many countries bilateral or multilateral trade deals that held fast to the original neoliberal promise to eliminate or reduce existing trade barriers among nations. Similarly, the Trump administration's much publicized trade deal to replace NAFTA with USMCA amounts to little more than NAFTA 2.0—a cosmetic update that retains much of the original framework worked out by the second-wave neoliberal Clinton administration in the early 1990s.

In short, our assessment of Trumpism reveals a messy ideological mixture that advances some core principles of economic nationalism while also furthering significant items of the neoliberal agenda. For this reason, it might be apt to characterize his economic stance in contradictory terms as 'nationalist neoliberalism', or, as other commentators have suggested, as 'authoritarian neoliberalism'. While this contradictory concept indicates that neoliberalism is now suffering from a deepening legitimation crisis that has buoyed the fortunes of national populism, it also reveals the uncanny staying power of some major neoliberal tenets.

**Table 4. Examples of Donald Trump's Neoliberal Executive Orders (2017–19)**

| EO number, year of issue, and title | Affected policy area(s) | Mandated changes | Involved neoliberal norms |
|---|---|---|---|
| 13771 (2017): Reducing Regulation and Controlling Regulatory Costs | All domestic and foreign policies | For every new regulation issued by government agency, at least two prior regulations must be eliminated | Deregulation; reduction of public spending; downsizing government |
| 13783 (2017): Promoting Energy Independence and Economic Growth | Energy, environment, security | Suspend, revise, or rescind existing regulations that burden the development or use of domestically produced energy resources | Deregulation; privatization; enticement of foreign investment; enforcement of property and private landownership |
| 13812 (2017): Revocation of EO Creating Labour Management Forums | Labour | Revoke Obama-era EO13522 to create labour-management forums to improve delivery of government services | Restriction of labour/union organization; secure labour 'flexibility' |
| 13828 (2018): Reducing Poverty in America by Promoting Opportunity and Economic Mobility | Social (welfare), housing, family | Clear paths to self-sufficiency by cutting public assistance programmes and moving poor people into the workforce | Reduction of public spending though reduction of social services and welfare programmes; replace welfare with 'workfare'; privatization of public services; downsizing government |

*(Continued)*

**Table 4. (Continued)**

| EO number, year of issue, and title | Affected policy area(s) | Mandated changes | Involved neoliberal norms |
|---|---|---|---|
| 13836 (2018): Developing Efficient, Effective, and Cost-Reducing Approaches to Federal Sector Collective Bargaining | Labour | Encourage highest levels of employee performance on the job, cut taxpayer-funded union negotiation time, and preserve management rights to achieve more efficient outcomes in collective bargaining processes | Restriction of labour/union organization; secure labour 'flexibility'; reduction of public spending |
| 13872 (2019): Economic Empowerment of Asian Americans and Pacific Islanders (AAPI) | All economic policies | Establish Presidential Commission on AAPI to develop strategies for encouraging innovation and entrepreneurship in AAPI communities | Promotion of entrepreneurship and market-oriented enterprises; expansion of neoliberal logic to 'disadvantaged' groups |
| 13878 (2019): Establish a White House Council on Eliminating Regulatory Barriers to Affordable Housing | Housing, transportation, environment, labour, tax | Eliminate regulatory 'barriers' on housing industry such as 'burdensome' zoning and growth management controls and rent controls; 'excessive' wetland and environment regulations; and tax policies that discourage investment | Deregulation; privatization of public services; reduction of taxes; downsizing government |

*Source*: US Federal Register (2019: <http://www.federalregister.gov/presidential-documents/executive-orders/donald-trump>.

# Final reflections: the demise or rebirth of neoliberalism?

Having almost reached the end of our journey through the diverse landscapes of neoliberalism, let us conclude this book with a brief speculation on the future of neoliberalism by focusing on our core questions raised in the Preface. Is neoliberalism doomed or will it regain its former glory? Might a new version of neoliberalism succeed in drowning out the siren song of national-populism and its nostalgic promise to return to the good old days of territorial sovereignty and national greatness? If so, what might such a new neoliberalism look like?

There seem to be two possible future scenarios for neoliberalism. The first is predicated upon a further intensification of the current national populist backlash and the strengthening of economic nationalism at the expense of neoliberalism. After all, populist leaders like President Trump see global trade as a zero-sum game between self-interested nations. Thus, they are prepared to impose steep tariffs on goods and services in order to reduce their country's trade deficit. If nationalist leaders like Trump or Prime Minister Boris Johnson further increase their political power, one could easily imagine a proliferation of trade wars that might draw many countries and regions into their orbit. As a result, consumers—especially those located in the more prosperous global North—would not only have to put up with higher prices for many commodities and services, but also face the likelihood of the intensifying trade war adversely affecting the health of the entire world economy.

The chaotic Brexit process and the first term of the Trump presidency are instructive examples of how the national populist surge can weaken representative democracy and liberal values that underpin neoliberalism. If the promises of neoliberals continue to run afoul of the reality of runaway inequality and the perceived loss of national traditions and cultural identity, people will blame the remaining governing neoliberal elites usually affiliated with established mainstream parties. The result would be a further loss of legitimacy of neoliberalism in all of its dimensions: as an ideology, as a mode of governance, and as a policy package. Indeed, it might even spell the end of neoliberalism as a particular form of free-market capitalism that dominated the world for four decades.

The second possible future trajectory of neoliberalism is built on the possibility of massive and enduring losses of antiglobalist populists at the ballot box, thus indicating the cresting of the populist wave and the return of a neoliberal free-market outlook. Such a rebound scenario would enhance the tendencies of the third wave of neoliberalism we discussed in Chapter 2. Indeed, the programmatic outline of such a neoliberalism with a high-tech face has recently been discussed at important ideological sites of global capitalism such as the World Economic Forum (WEF). Built upon claims of the touted benefits of digital globalization, the new neoliberal vision has been heavily promoted by Klaus Schwab.

The German founder and executive chairman of the WEF has asserted that the world finds itself today in the throes of a 'fourth industrial revolution'—the complete digitization of the social, political, and economic sectors. Thus, Schwab predicts a transformation of existing social structures in profound ways that would blur the lines between physical, digital, and biological spheres. Admitting that the free-market consensus of the consecutive waves of neoliberalism has been smashed by the populist surge and might be beyond repair, the WEF boss believes that neoliberalism can be reformed by means of the new leading technologies of the 21st century such as artificial intelligence, autonomous vehicles, quantum computing, 3D printing, telecommuting, and the Internet of Things.

However, there remain serious issues with this rosy scenario of a new digital neoliberalism. These include the widening gap between winners and losers of the ICT revolution, the digitized spread of misinformation through social media, and the increasing reliance on robots and algorithms in all spheres of life. As we noted in Chapter 2, many experts warn that digital technology not only creates conveniences, but also eliminates millions of jobs through automation. The combination of neoliberal globalization and robotics might create what economist Richard Baldwin has called a 'globotics upheaval' that threatens to disrupt the economy and overwhelm society's capacity to adapt. Former Harvard Business School Dean Shoshana Zuboff has pointed to another downside: the rise of 'surveillance capitalism' by means of new exploitative practices of corporate digital giants like Google and Facebook who unilaterally claim human experience as free material for translation into behavioural data designed to fuel and shape consumerist desires towards profitable outcomes.

Regardless of which scenario materializes, it is highly unlikely that our unsettled era will end any time soon. The years and decades ahead will bring new and unforeseen challenges. Still, as we have emphasized throughout this book, neoliberalism has shown a high degree of flexibility. Moreover, it comes in many forms and varieties, which enhances its remarkable ability to adapt to specific contexts and react to particular crises and opportunities. At the moment, it seems that neoliberalism has finally found its match in national populism. But it is entirely conceivable that new strands of neoliberalism—the two leading candidates being authoritarian neoliberalism and digital neoliberalism—will rise to dominance in our 21st-century world that faces serious global problems such as global climate change, new pandemics, and escalating inequality.

# References and further reading

As one would expect, there is an extensive literature on neoliberalism and related themes. But most of these books and articles are not easily accessible to those who are just setting out to acquire some knowledge of the subject. Having digested the contents of the present introduction, however, most readers will find themselves equipped to move on to some of the academic works listed below. Following the overall organization of Oxford's *Very Short Introduction* series, however, we have kept direct quotations to a minimum and indicated their source either immediately with the textboxes in which they appear or in this reference section. That said, we also wish to acknowledge our intellectual debt to the authors below, whose influence on the arguments of this book is not always obvious from the text.

## Preface

For an excellent discussion of the origin and various uses of the term 'neoliberalism' in academic social science literature, see Taylor C. Boas and Jordan Gans-Morse, 'Neoliberalism: From New Liberal Philosophy to Anti-Liberal Slogan', *Studies in Comparative International Development* 44/2 (June 2009), pp. 137–61.

## Chapter 1: What's 'neo' about liberalism?

Two excellent accounts of neoliberalism are David Harvey, *A Brief History of Neoliberalism* (Oxford University Press, 2005); and David M. Kotz, *The Rise and Fall of Neoliberalism* (Harvard University Press, 2015). For the role of ideas in neoliberalism, see Ravi K. Roy, Arthur T. Denzau, and Thomas D. Willett (eds), *Neoliberalism: National and Regional Experiments with Global Ideas* (Routledge, 2006).

Accessible books on classical liberalism include: Robert L. Heilbroner, *The Worldly Philosophers: The Lives, Times, and Ideas of the Great Economic Thinkers* (Touchstone, 1999); and Jerry Z. Muller, *The Mind and the Market: Capitalism in Modern European Thought* (Alfred A. Knopf, 2002).

For materials related to the economic ideas of John Maynard Keynes and Friedrich von Hayek, see Alan Ebenstein, *Hayek's Journey: The Mind of Friedrich Hayek* (Palgrave Macmillan, 2003); Nicholas Wapshott, *Keynes Hayek: The Clash That Defined Modern Economics* (W. W. Norton, 2012); and Quinn Slobodian, *Globalists: The End of Empire and the Birth of Neoliberalism* (Harvard University Press, 2018). For the crucial role played by Keynes in setting up the post-war international economic order, see Benn Steil, *The Battle of Bretton Woods: John Maynard Keynes, Harry Dexter White and the Making of a New World Order* (Princeton University Press, 2014).

The source for materials included in Box 3 can be found in Robert Reich, *Supercapitalism: The Transformation of Business, Democracy, and Everyday Life* (Knopf, 2008), p. 17.

For representative surveys and histories of political ideologies, see Michael Freeden, *Ideology: A Very Short Introduction* (Oxford University Press, 2009); and Manfred B. Steger, *The Rise of the Global Imaginary: Political Ideologies from the French Revolution to the Global War on Terror* (Oxford University Press, 2008).

The full transcript of Donald Trump's remarks at the 2018 joint press conference with Shinzō Abe is available at: <https://factba.se/transcript/donald-trump-press-conference-shinzo-abe-japan-june-7-2018>.

For the quotes related to the National Conservatism Conference in Washington, DC (14–16 July 2019), see Jennifer Schuessler, 'Polishing the Nationalist Brand in the Trump Era', *New York Times* (19 July 2019): <https://www.nytimes.com/2019/07/19/arts/trump-nationalism-tucker-carlson.html>.

## Chapter 2: Three waves of neoliberalism

For further readings on Reaganomics and Thatcherism, see William A. Niskanen, *Reaganomics: An Insider's Account of the*

*Policies and the People* (Oxford University Press, 1988); Richard Heffernan, *New Labour and Thatcherism*: *Political Change in Britain* (St Martin's Press, 2000); Eric J. Evans, *Thatcher and Thatcherism* (Routledge, 2004); and Monica Prasad, *The Politics of Free Markets*: *The Rise of Neoliberal Economic Policies in Britain, France, Germany, and the United States* (University of Chicago Press, 2006).

For two opposing ideological perspectives on neoconservatism, see Irving Kristol, *Neoconservatism*: *The Autobiography of an Idea* (Ivan R. Dee, 1999); and John Ehrenberg, *Servants of Wealth*: *The Right's Attack on Economic Justice* (Rowman & Littlefield, 2006). Opposing treatments of economic nationalism include Eric Helleiner and Andreas Pickel (eds), *Economic Nationalism in a Globalizing World* (Cornell University Press, 2005); and Stephen Moore and Arthur Laffer, *Trumponomics: Inside the America First Plan to Get Our Economy Back on Track* (All Points Books, 2018).

We suggest the following further readings on Clinton's market globalism and Tony Blair's Third Way: Michael Meeropol, *Surrender*: *How the Clinton Administration Completed the Reagan Revolution* (University of Michigan Press, 1998); Anthony Giddens, *The Global Third Way Debate* (Polity, 2001); and Matt Beech and Simon Lee (eds), *Ten Years of New Labour* (Palgrave Macmillan, 2008).

Our discussion of anti-trust policy in the Clinton era relies in part on Robert E. Litan and Carl Shapiro, 'Anti-Trust Policy in the Clinton Administration', in Jeffrey Frankel and Peter Orszag (eds), *American Economic Policy in the 1990s* (Massachusetts Institute of Technology Press, 2002).

For a discussion of past and present globalization dynamics, see Manfred B. Steger, *Globalization*: *A Very Short Introduction*, 5th edn (Oxford University Press, 2020); and Manfred B. Steger and Paul James, *Globalization Matters: Engaging the Global in Unsettled Times* (Cambridge University Press, 2019).

For more detail on NPM, see Robert B. Denhardt, *Theories of Public Organization*, 7th edn (Wadsworth, 2014). Box 8 summarizes information on 'neoliberal institutionalism' that appears in Philip Cerny, 'Embedding Neoliberalism: The Evolution of a Hegemonic Paradigm', *Journal of International Trade and Diplomacy* 2/1 (2008), pp. 1–46.

Our summary of the influence of neoliberal think tanks relies in part on Otto Singer, 'Knowledge and Politics in Economic

Policy-Making: Official Economic Advisers in the USA, Britain and Germany', in B. Guy Peters and Anthony Barker (eds), *Advising West European Governments: Inquiries, Expertise and Public Policy* (Edinburgh University Press, 1993). On the growing power of think tanks, see James G. McGann, *The Fifth Estate: Think Tanks, Public Policy, and Governance* (The Brookings Institution Press, 2016).

The quote pertaining to 'anonymous markets. . .' in the third-wave neoliberal era is extracted from John Kay, *Other People's Money: The Real Business of Finance* (PublicAffairs, 2015). Our discussion of 'financialization' in the third-wave neoliberal era was drawn from Ravi K. Roy and Thomas D. Willett, 'Financialization', in Mark Juergensmeyer, Saskia Sassen, and Manfred B. Steger (eds), *The Oxford Handbook of Global Studies* (Oxford University Press, 2019).

## Chapter 3: Neoliberalism in the Asia-Pacific Region

For the classical account of the Asian development model in the context of Japan, see Chalmers Johnson, *MITI and the Japanese Miracle: The Growth of Industrial Policy, 1925–1975* (Stanford University Press, 1982). The model's application to Taiwan, South Korea, and other newly industrializing countries is outlined in Robert Wade, *Governing the Market: Economic Theory and the Role of Government in East Asian Industrialization* (Princeton University Press, 1990).

Additional useful accounts of neoliberalization dynamics in Asia include: *The East Asian Miracle: Economic Growth and Public Policy*, A World Bank Policy Research Report (Oxford University Press, 1993); Jagdish Bhagwati, *India in Transition: Freeing the Economy* (Oxford University Press, 1993); Aurelia George Mulgan, *Japan's Failed Revolution: Koizumi and the Politics of Economic Reform* (Asia Pacific Press, 2002); Arvind Panagariya, 'India in the 1980s and 1990s: A Triumph of Reforms', *IMF Working Paper*, WP/04/43, 2004; Aihwa Ong, *Neoliberalism as Exception: Mutations in Citizenship and Sovereignty* (Duke University Press, 2006); Bae-Goon Park, Richard Child Hill, and Asato Saito (eds), *Locating Neoliberalism in Asia: Neoliberalizing Spaces on Development States* (Wiley-Blackwell, 2011); Quan Li, *The Idea of Governance and the Spirit of Chinese Neoliberalism* (Palgrave Macmillan, 2018).

Our discussion of Chinese SOEs leans on David Harvey, *A Brief History of Neoliberalism* (Oxford University Press, 2005).

## Chapter 4: Neoliberalism in Latin America and Africa

Our discussion in this chapter has greatly benefited from the arguments made by Naomi Klein, *The Shock Doctrine*: *The Rise of Disaster Capitalism* (Penguin Books, 2007). We also drew on useful ideas and arguments presented in: Anil Hira, *Ideas and Economic Policy in Latin America*: *Regional, National, and Organizational Case Studies* (Praeger, 1998) and *An East Asian Model for Latin American Success*: *The New Path* (Ashgate, 2007); J. L. Adedeji, 'The Legacy of J. J. Rawlings in Ghanaian Politics', *African Studies Quarterly* 5 (2001): online at: <http://web.africa.ufl.edu/asq/v5/v5i2a1.htm>; Dominick Salvatore, James W. Dean, and Thomas D. Willett (eds), *The Dollarization Debate* (Oxford University Press, 2003); Sarah Babb, *Managing Mexico*: *Economists from Nationalism to Neoliberalism* (Princeton University Press, 2004); and James Ferguson, *Global Shadows*: *Africa in the Neoliberal World Order* (Duke University Press, 2006).

A radical, but riveting, account of the imposition of the Washington Consensus on the global South can be found in: John Perkins, *Confessions of an Economic Hit Man* (Penguin, 2005).

## Chapter 5: Neoliberalism challenged

For a description and analysis of the challengers of market globalism on the political Left and Right, see Manfred B. Steger, *Globalisms*: *Facing the Populist Challenge* (Rowman & Littlefield, 2020).

The source for information appearing in Box 16 can be found in Osama bin Laden, 'The Towers of Lebanon' (29 October 2004), in *Messages to the World: The Statements of Osama Bin Laden*, edited by Bruce Lawrence and translated by James Howarth (London: Verso, 2005), p. 242.

Our quotations of Donald Trump's public remarks are taken from two sources: (a) the American Presidency Project website: <http://presidency.ucsb.edu/2016_election.php>, an authoritative archive for the study of presidential speeches; and (b) the Factbase website: <http://factba.se>, a useful online source for the study of Trump's speeches, tweets, and video materials.

References and further reading

For an extended analysis of Trump's campaign speeches from which all
the direct quotes in this chapter are taken, see Manfred B. Steger,
'Mapping Antiglobalist Populism: Bringing Ideology Back In',
*Populism* 2 (2019), pp. 110–36.

For a comprehensive assessment of 'authoritarian neoliberalism', see
Jamie Peck and Nik Theodore, 'Still Neoliberalism?', *South Atlantic
Quarterly* 118/2 (April 2019), pp. 245–65.

For a readable account of the connections between neoliberalism and
Trumpism, see T. J. Coles, *President Trump, Inc: How Big Business
and Neoliberalism Empower Populism and the Far-Right*
(Clairview Books, 2017).

Insightful recent accounts of the impact of authoritarian populism on
neoliberalism that contain speculations on its future include:
Wendy Brown, *In the Ruins of Neoliberalism: The Rise of
Antidemocratic Politics in the West* (Columbia University Press,
2019); Thomas Biebricher, *The Political Theory of Neoliberalism*
(Stanford University Press, 2019); and Adam Kotsko,
*Neoliberalism's Demons: On the Political Theology of Late
Capitalism* (Stanford University Press, 2018).

For an examination of the future of digital globalization and
automation, see Richard Baldwin, *The Globotics Upheaval:
Globalization, Robotics, and the Future of Work* (Oxford University
Press, 2019).

On the fascinating topic of 'surveillance capitalism', see Shoshana
Zuboff, *The Age of Surveillance Capitalism: The Fight for a Human
Future at the New Frontier of Power* (Public Affairs, 2019).

# Index

For the benefit of digital users, indexed terms that span two pages (e.g., 52–53) may, on occasion, appear on only one of those pages.

Neoliberalism

# GEOPOLITICS
## A Very Short Introduction
Klaus Dodds

In certain places such as Iraq or Lebanon, moving a few
feet either side of a territorial boundary can be a matter of life
or death, dramatically highlighting the connections between
place and politics. For a country's location and size as well as
its sovereignty and resources all affect how the people that live
there understand and interact with the wider world. Using
wide-ranging examples, from historical maps to James Bond
films and the rhetoric of political leaders like Churchill and
George W. Bush, this Very Short Introduction shows why,
for a full understanding of contemporary global politics, it is
not just smart - it is essential - to be geopolitical.

'Engrossing study of a complex topic.'

Mick Herron, Geographical.

# GLOBALIZATION
## A Very Short Introduction
Manfred Steger

'Globalization' has become one of the defining buzzwords of our time - a term that describes a variety of accelerating economic, political, cultural, ideological, and environmental processes that are rapidly altering our experience of the world. It is by its nature a dynamic topic - and this *Very Short Introduction* has been fully updated for 2009, to include developments in global politics, the impact of terrorism, and environmental issues. Presenting globalization in accessible language as a multifaceted process encompassing global, regional, and local aspects of social life, Manfred B. Steger looks at its causes and effects, examines whether it is a new phenomenon, and explores the question of whether, ultimately, globalization is a good or a bad thing.

www.oup.com/vsi